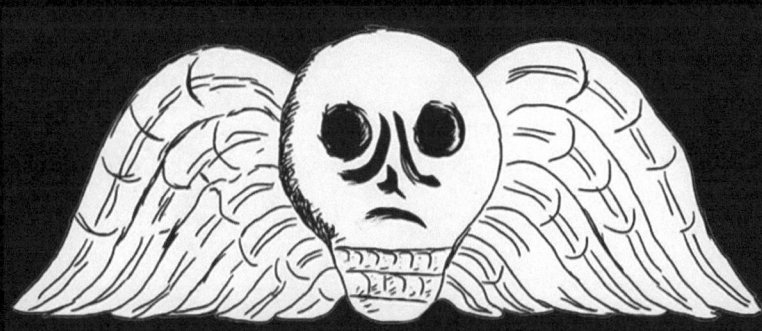

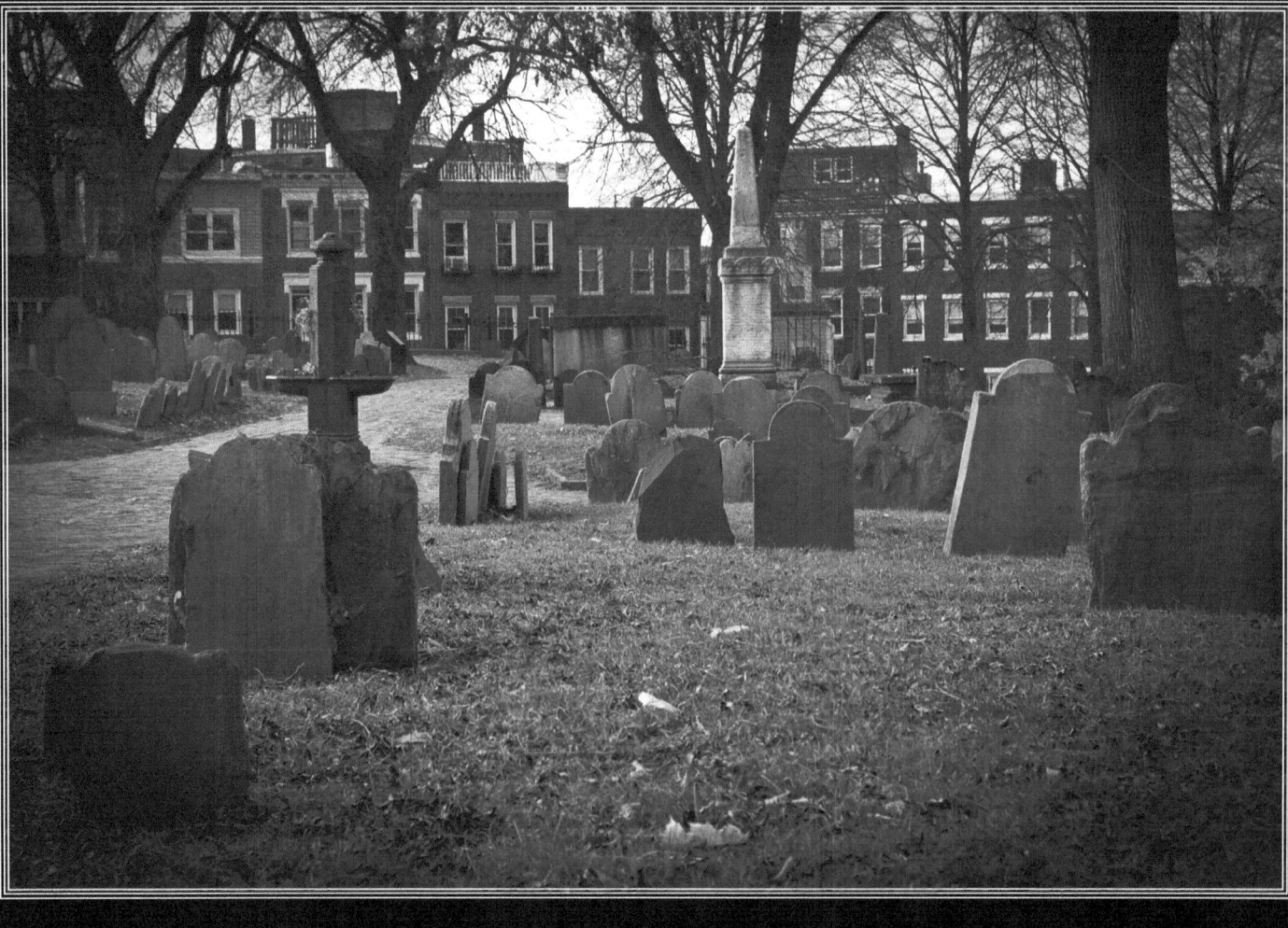

Copp's Hill Burying Ground is, in many ways, the cemetery by which all others are measured, not in calculations such as the size or grandeur of its grave markers but rather because, when we think of a graveyard, the basic characteristics present here are what come to mind. Even though it's in a densely populated part of Boston, it's not the easiest place to find and seems a remote location. It overlooks the harbor and the terrain is varied and uneven. Thousands are buried in this place, all the stones are at odd angles and sometimes, literally, on top of each other. The markers themselves are in disrepair and are beautifully illustrated with winged skulls, angelic faces and hand-chiseled designs. Ask any child to draw a tombstone and it's pretty certain you'll find something like that on *Copp's Hill*. It is both beautiful and creepy and incites the imagination and curiosity of anyone who finds themselves passing through its gates, transporting them into another era.

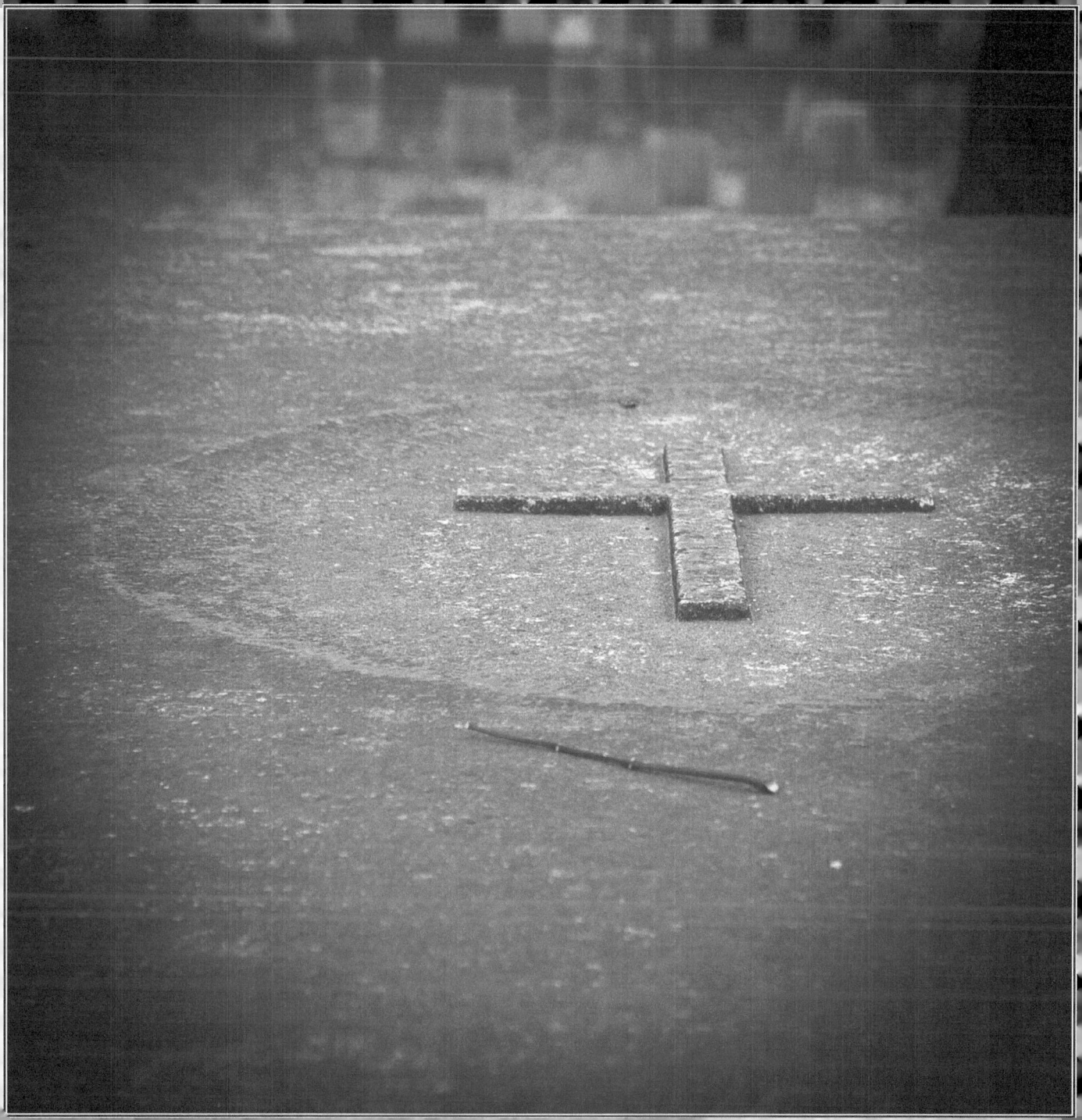

History

Copp's Hill is the second oldest burial ground in the city of Boston, founded in 1659 as Windmill Hill after a windmill that was located there. It was named after the cobbler, William Copp, and became the burial ground for many of the merchants, artists and craft people who lived in the North End. The land for the graveyard was given to the town and became the final resting place of thousands of people, warranting an addition in 1708 (from part of a pasture owned by the of daughter John Hull, master of the Boston mint) and another in 1809 (sold to the town for $10,000 by Benjamin Weld and his wife Nabby).

In addition to the local North Enders, thousands of African-Americans from the "New Guinea" neighborhood are buried at the base of the hill in unmarked graves along the Snowhill Street side. The Mather family of ministers and Edmund Hartt Robert Newman (who placed the lanterns in the Old North Church steeple for the Battle of Lexington and Concord), Prince Hall (the anti-slavery activist and founder of the Black Masonic Order) and Shem Drowne (who made the grasshopper weathervane on top of Faneuil Hall) are interred here.

Although the town continued to maintain the site now and then, by 1887 it had become badly neglected and almost forgotten despite its location in a well-populated area. It didn't helped the state of the grounds when the stones were used by British soldiers for target practice during the American Revolution. Additionally, stone and other materials were plundered by contractors over the years (mostly from the African-American sections it seems).

It was added to Boston's Freedom Trail tour and to the national Historic Register in 1974. Because of this, it is now protected and maintained... though the scars of years of neglect, bullets and graffiti are still clearly visible throughout.

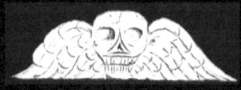

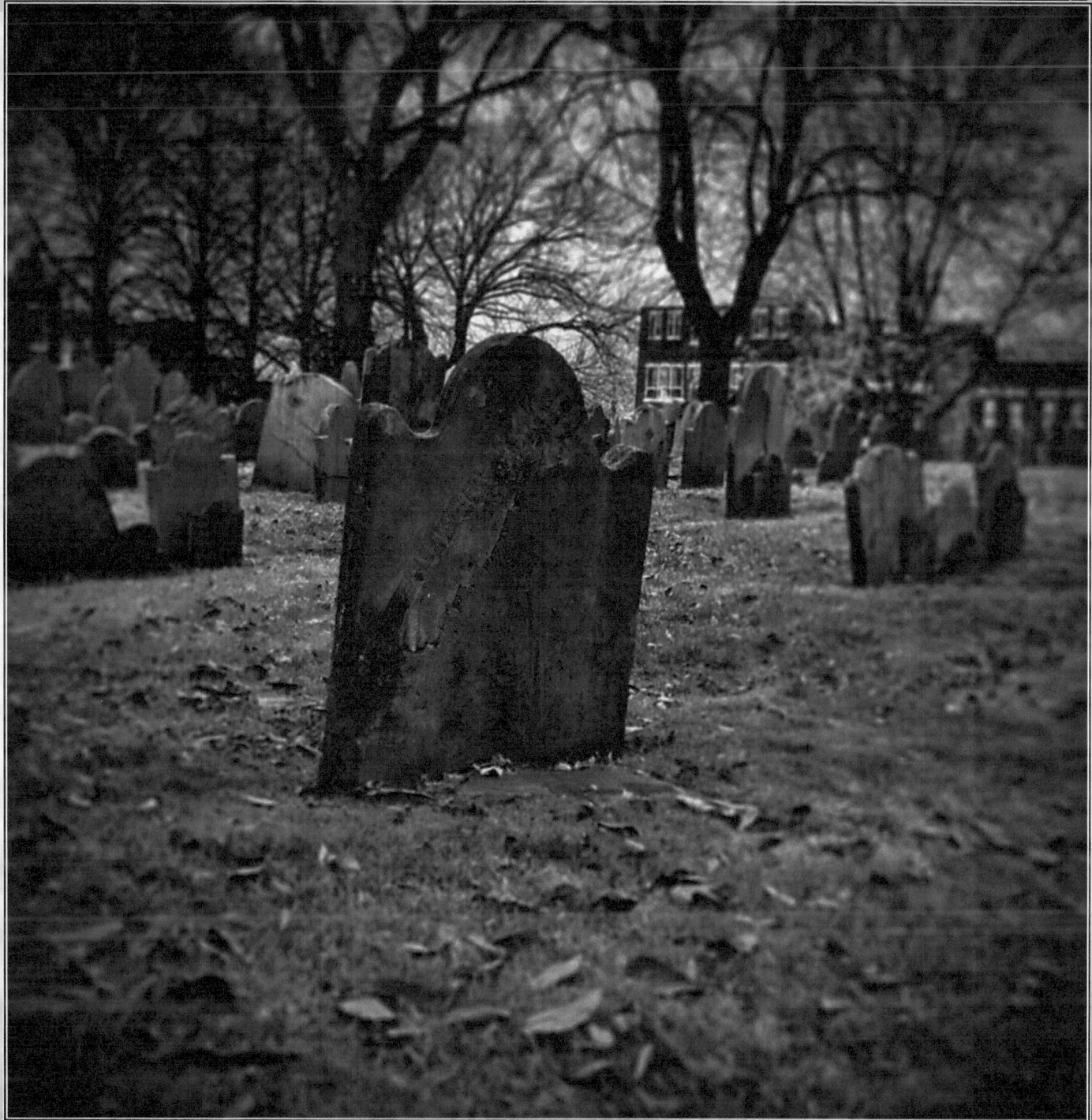

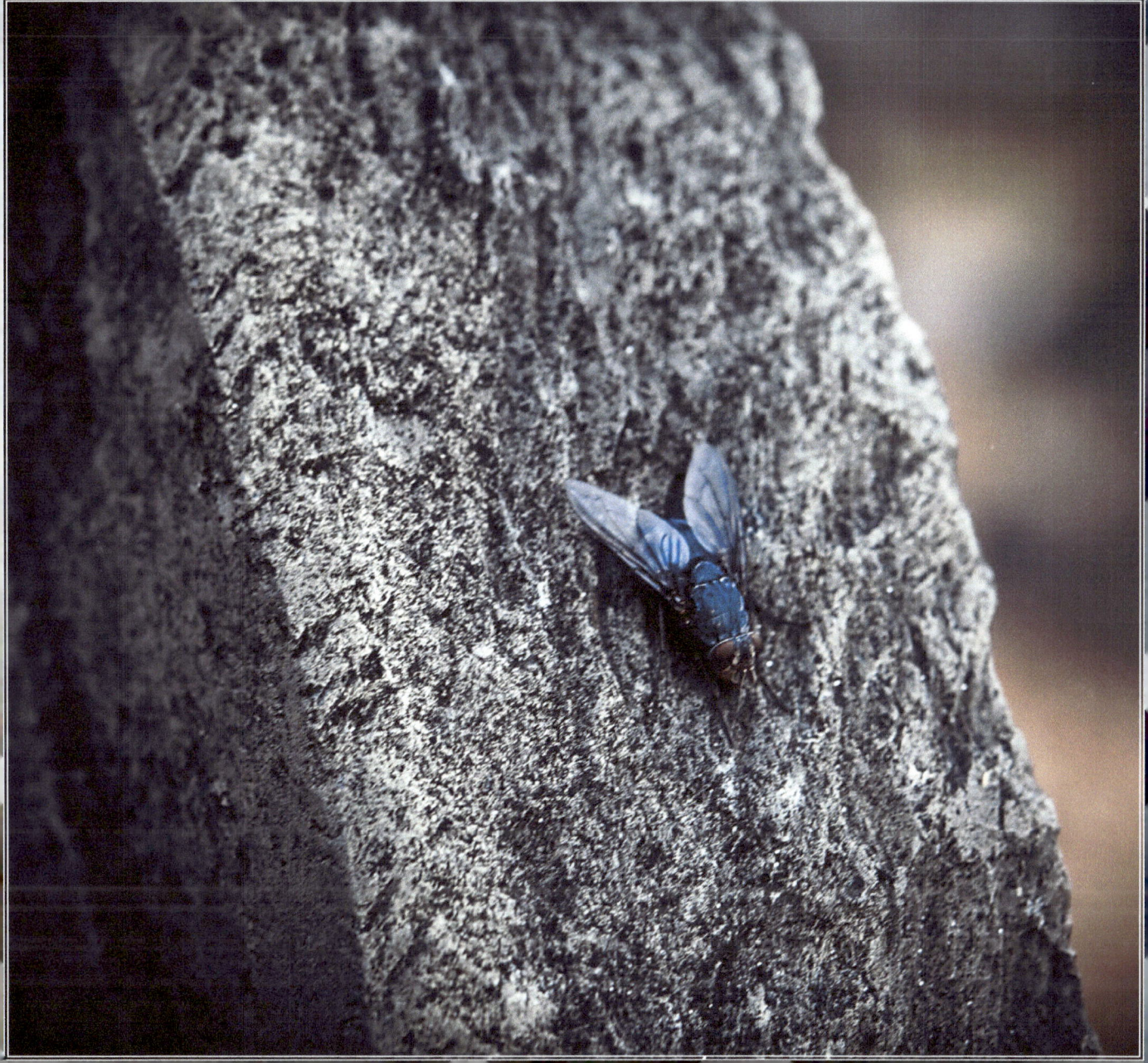

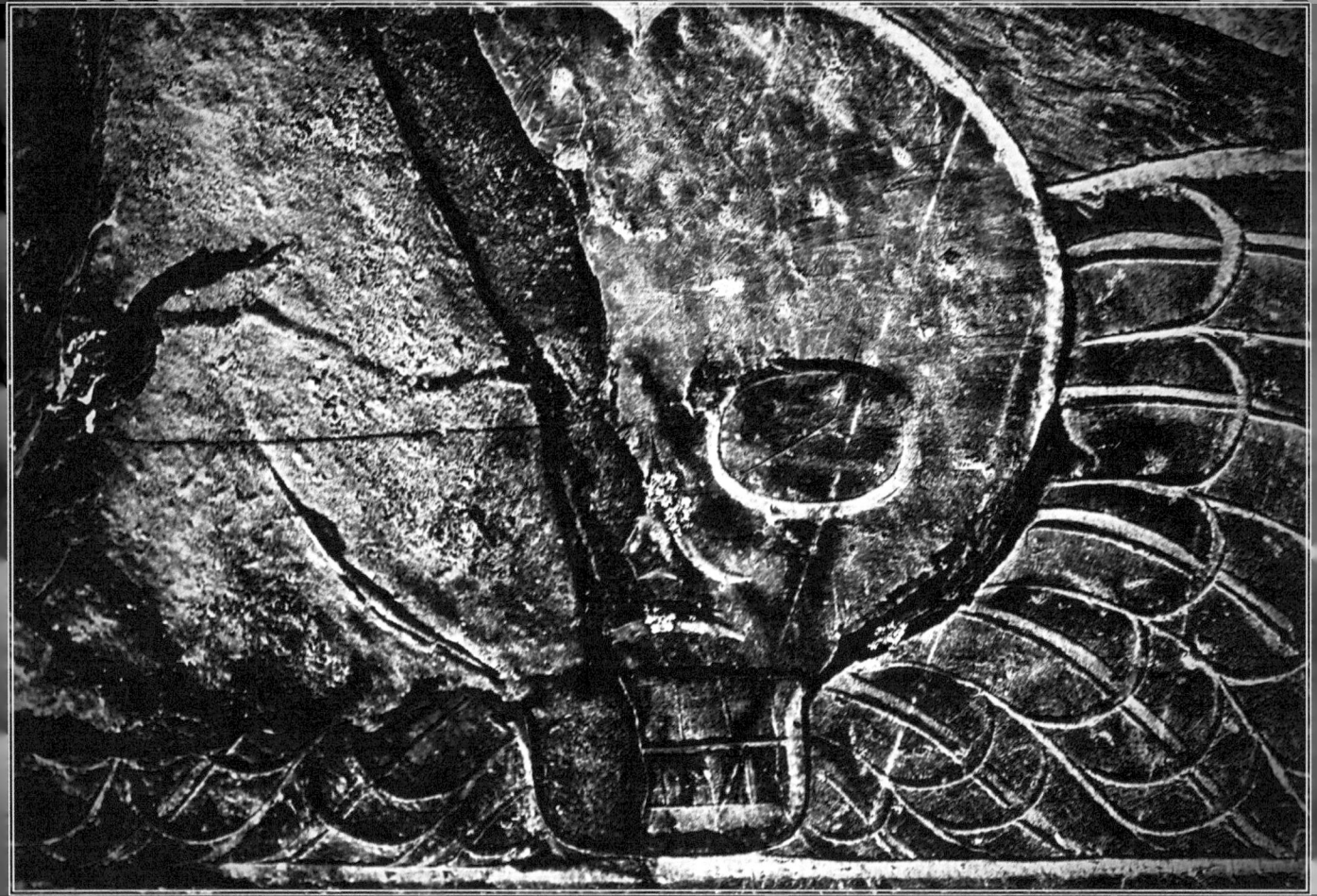

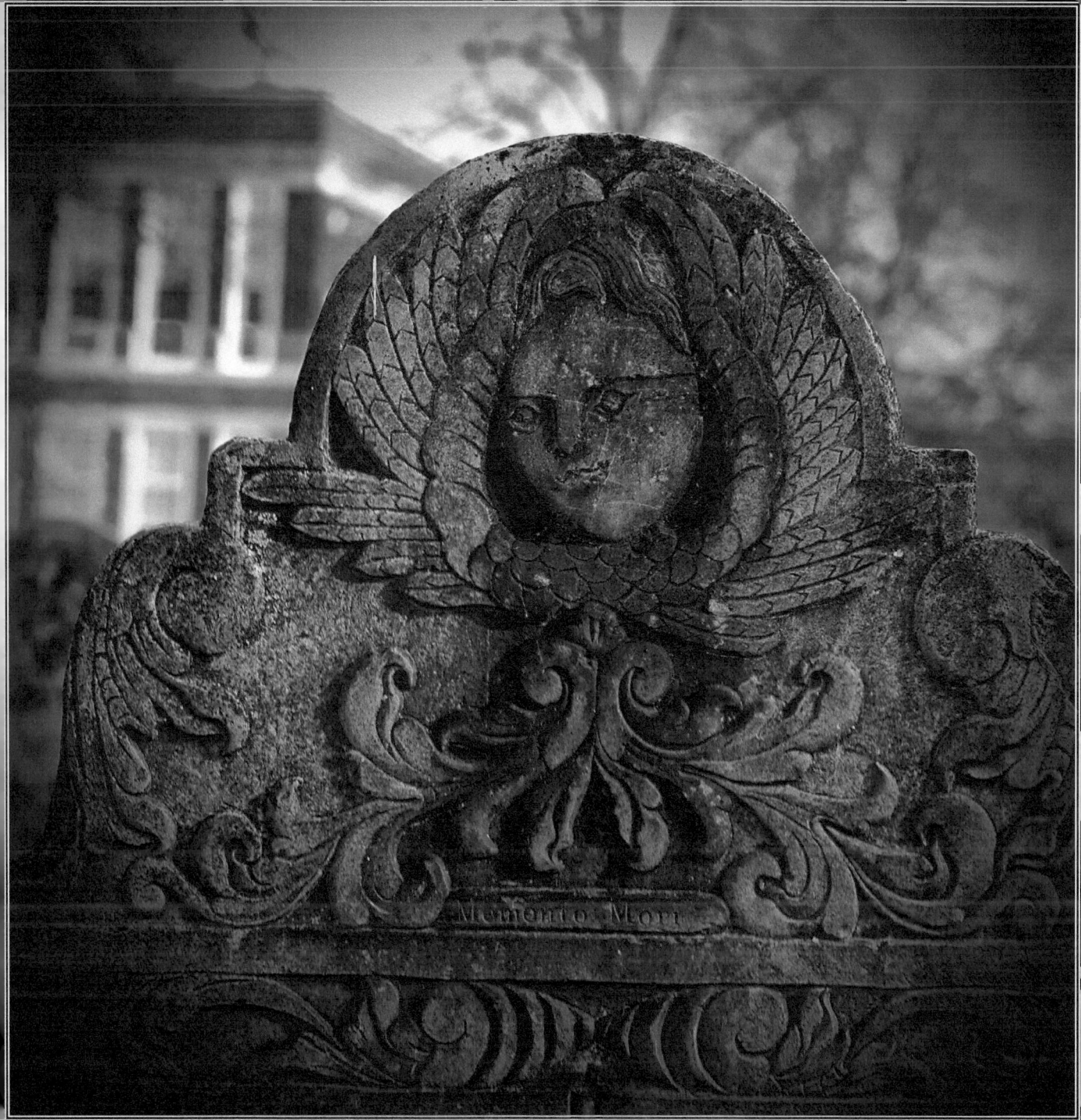
Memento Mori

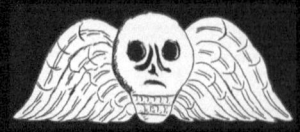

In Memory of ENOCH HOPKINS who
departed this life Dec 27, 1778 AE 55 years.

"Tell them tho' 'tis an awful thing to die,
T'was even to thee; yet the path once trod,
Heaven lifts its everlasting portals high,
And bids the pure in heart behold their God."

Sacred to the Memory of MRS BETSEY PITMAN
Wife to Mr. Joseph Pitman who departed this life March 8th 1784. Aged 27 years.

"Haste! Haste! He lyes in wait. He watches at the door.
Insidious Death! Should his strong hand arrest,
No composition sets the prisoner free.
Death's terror is the mountain faith removes.
'Tis faith disarms destruction.
Belyeve, and taste the pleasures of a God!
Belyeve, and look with triumph on the grave."

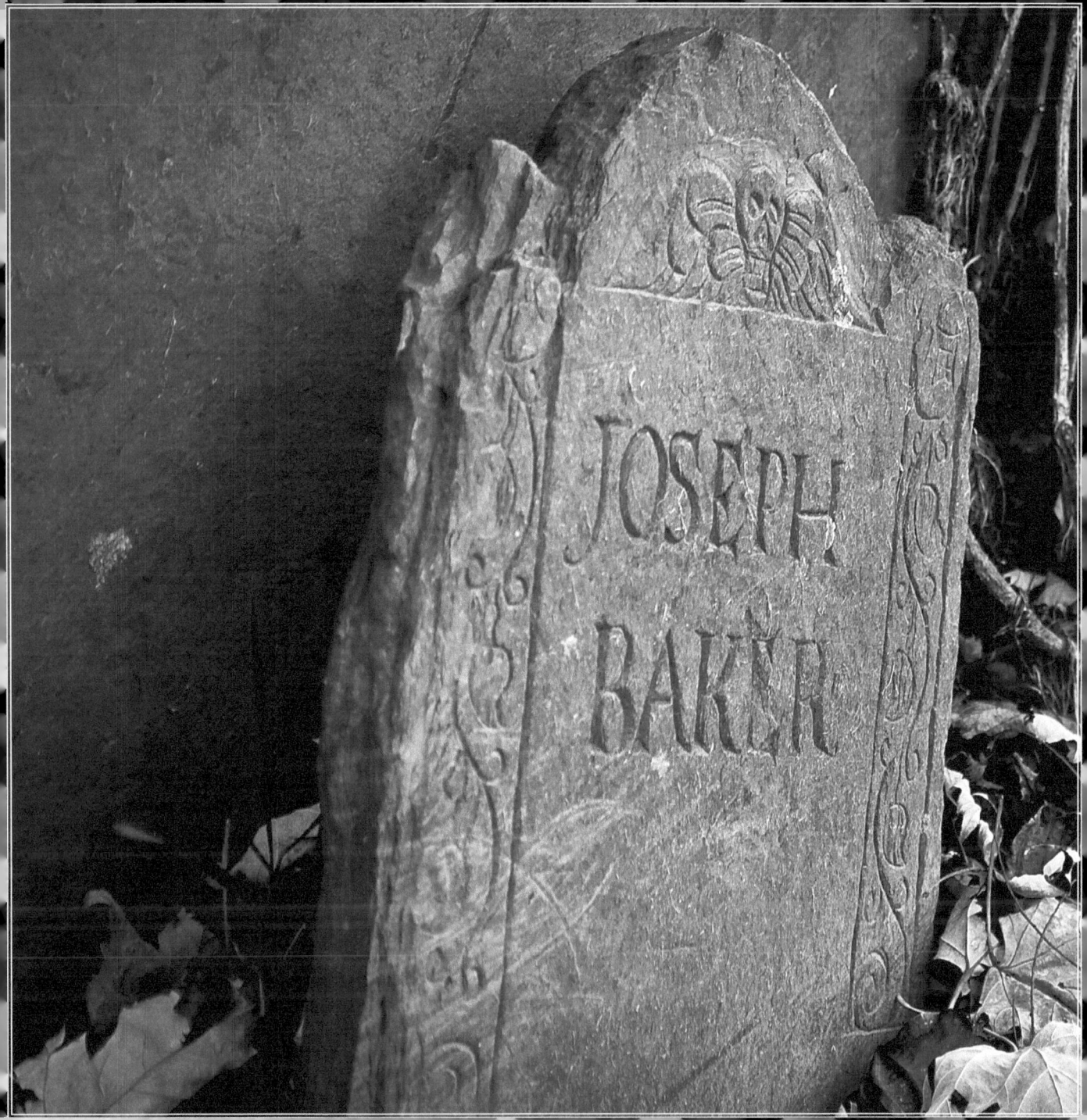

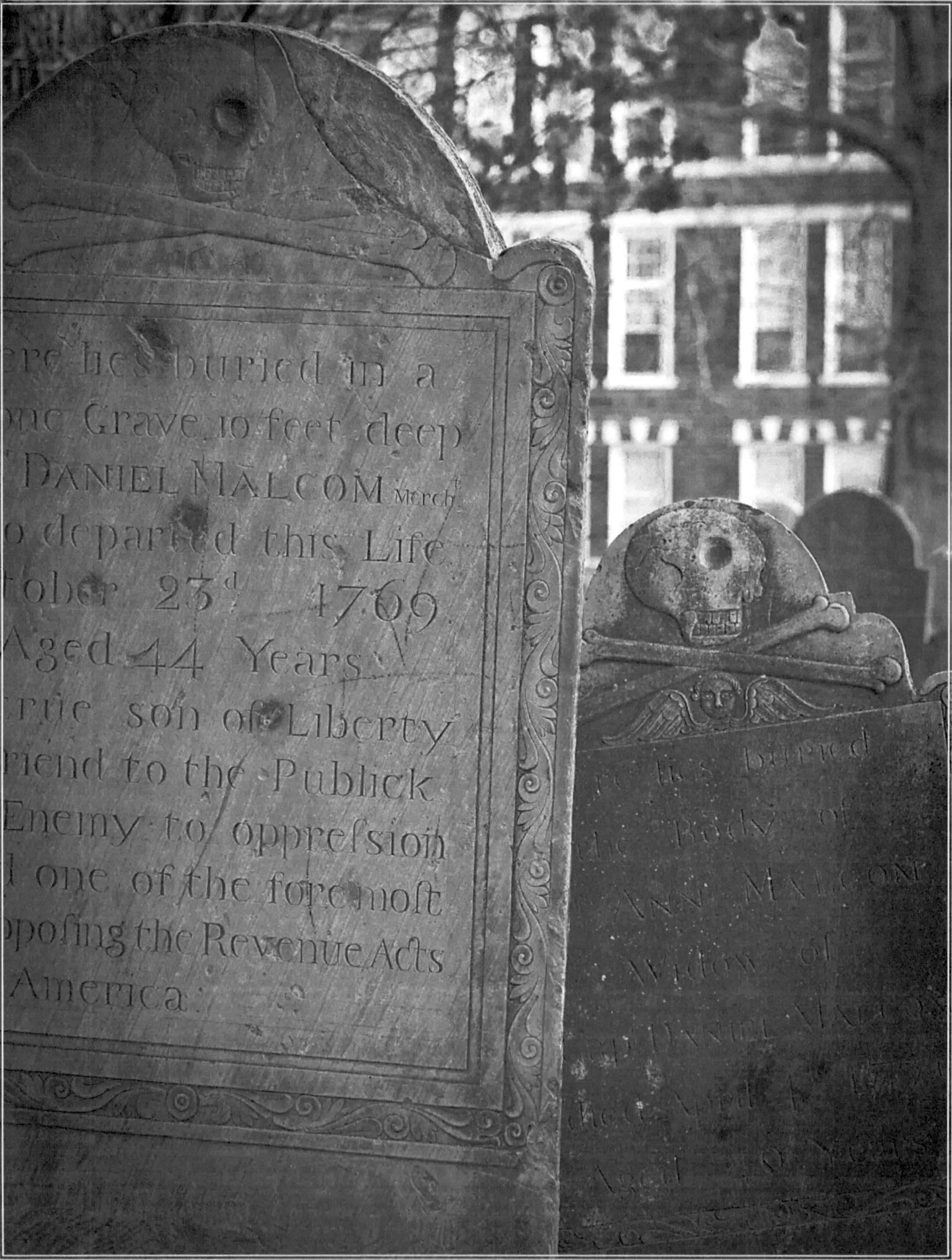

ere lies buried in a
one Grave 10 feet deep
DANIEL MALCOM Merch^t
o departed this Life
tober 23^d 1769
Aged 44 Years
rue son of Liberty
riend to the Publick
Enemy to oppresfion
one of the foremoſt
opoſing the Revenue Acts
America

is buried
Body of
ANN MALCOM
Widow of
D DANIEL MALCOM
Aged
Aged

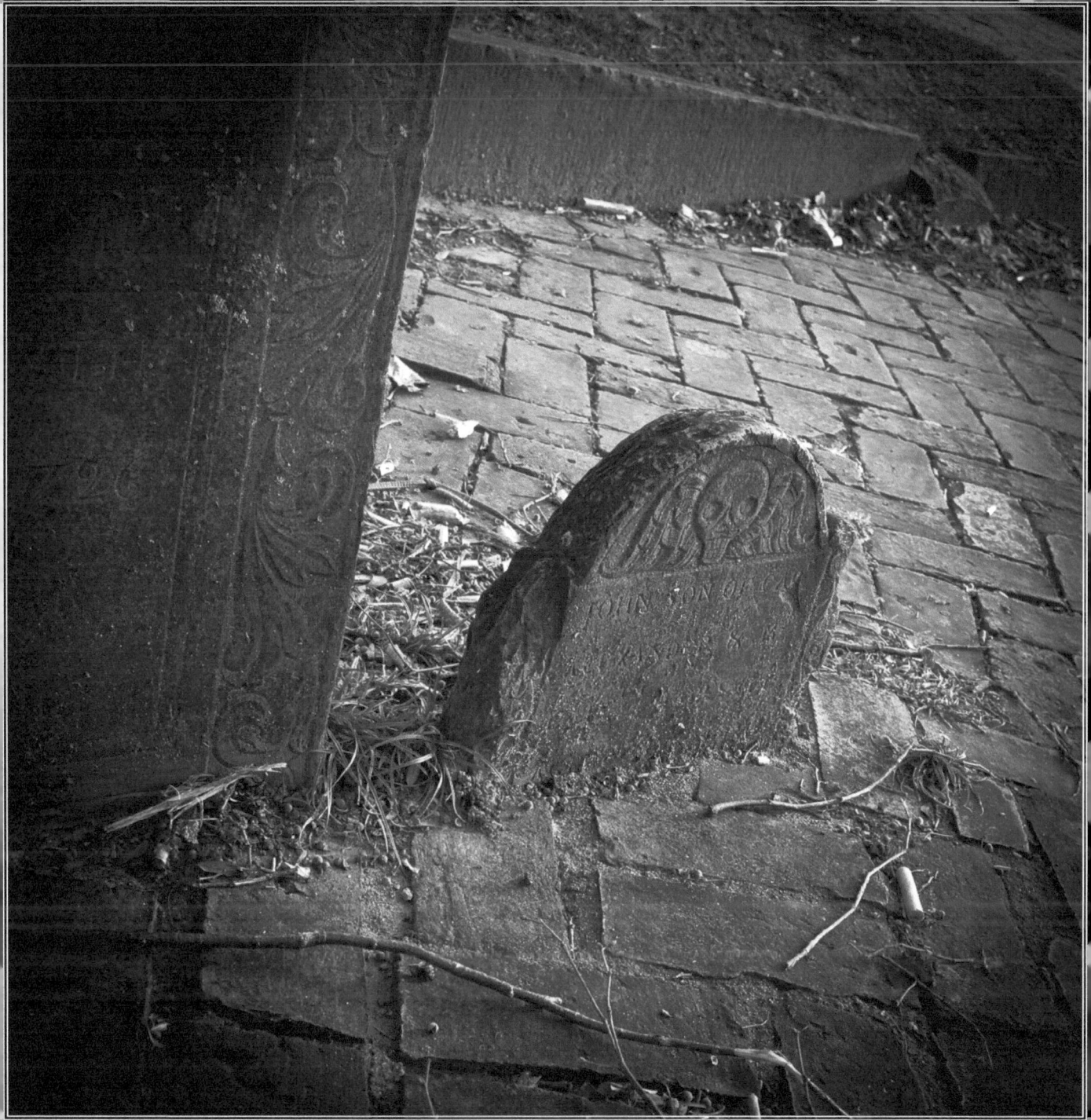

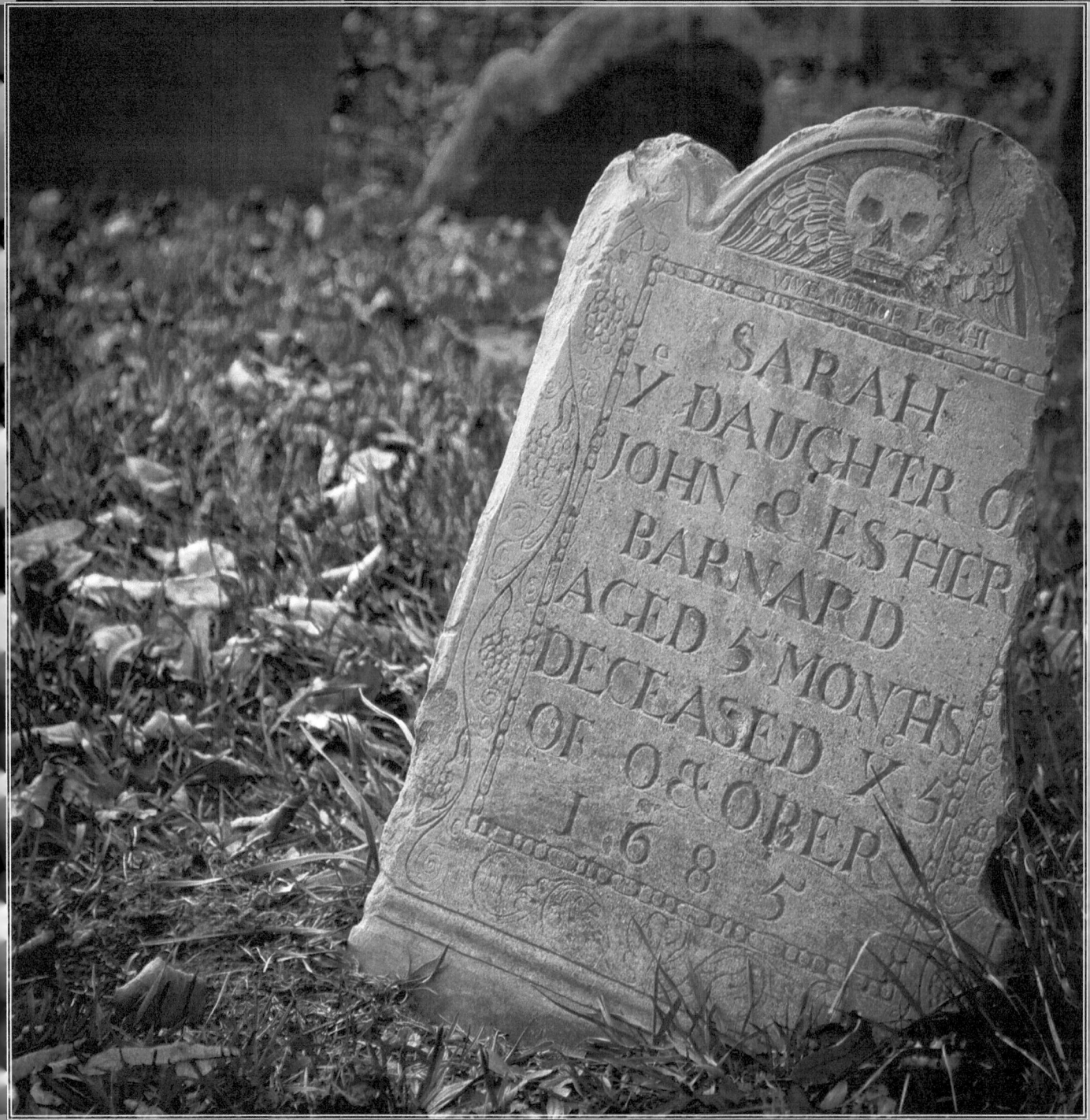

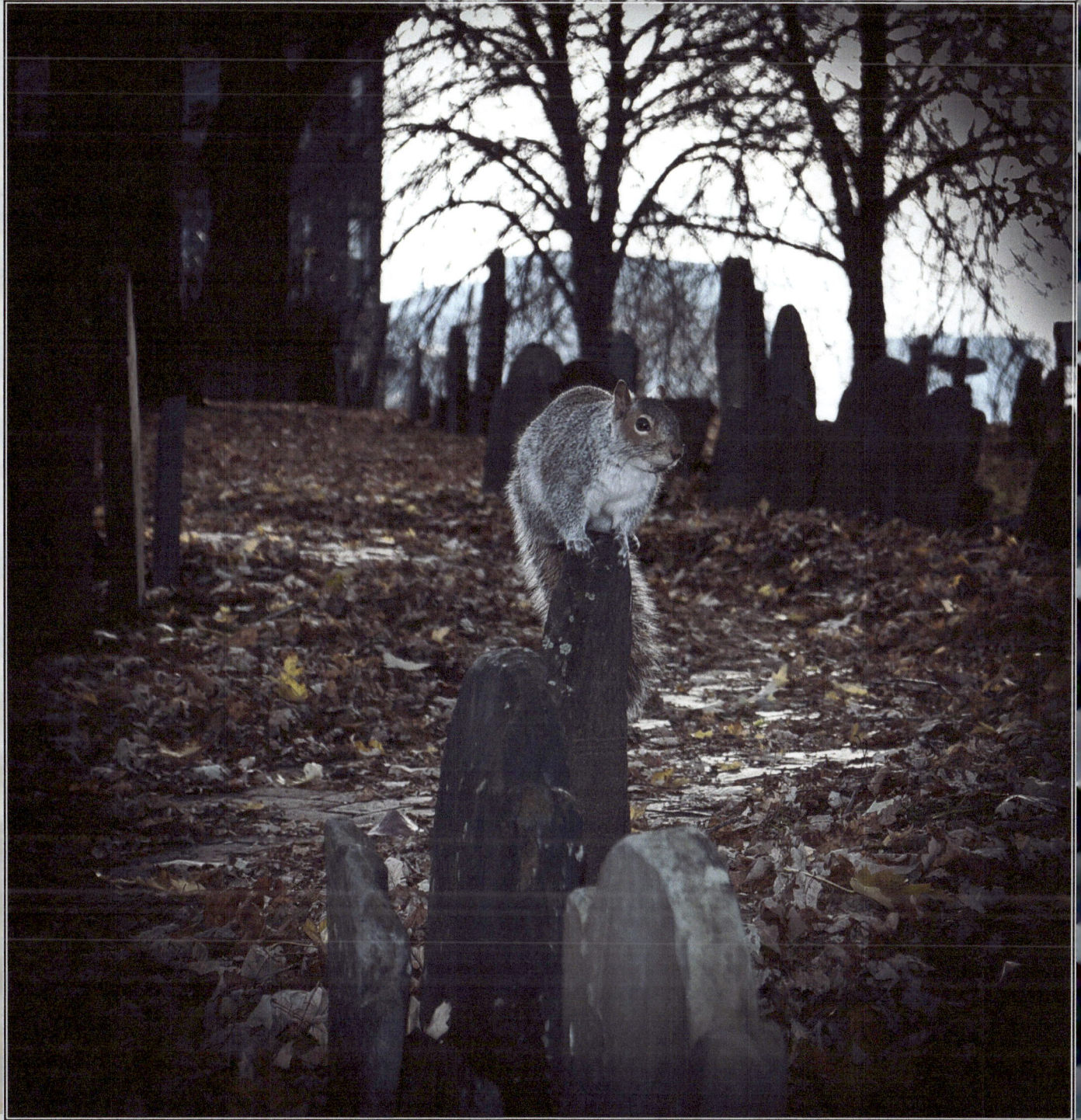

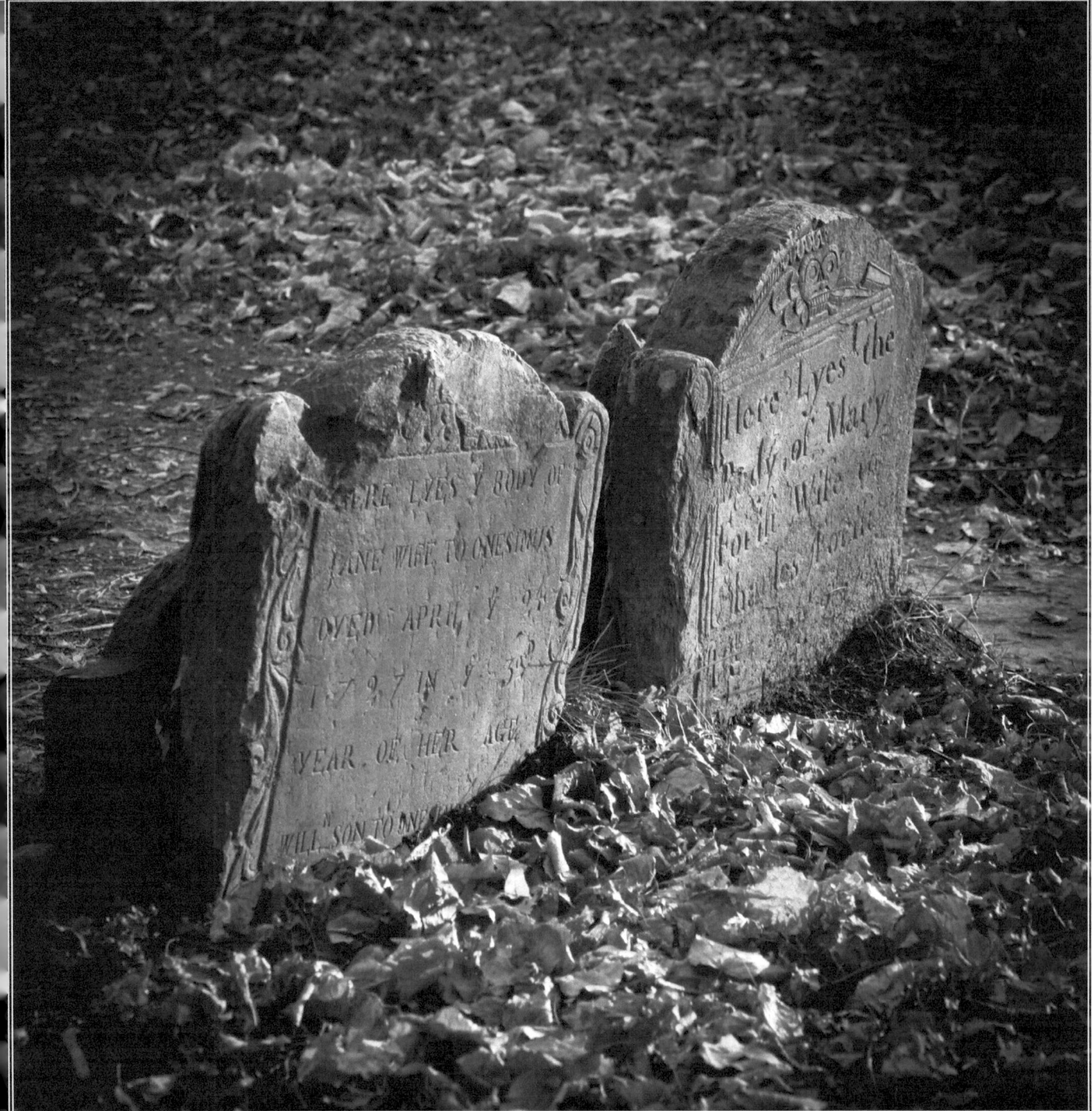

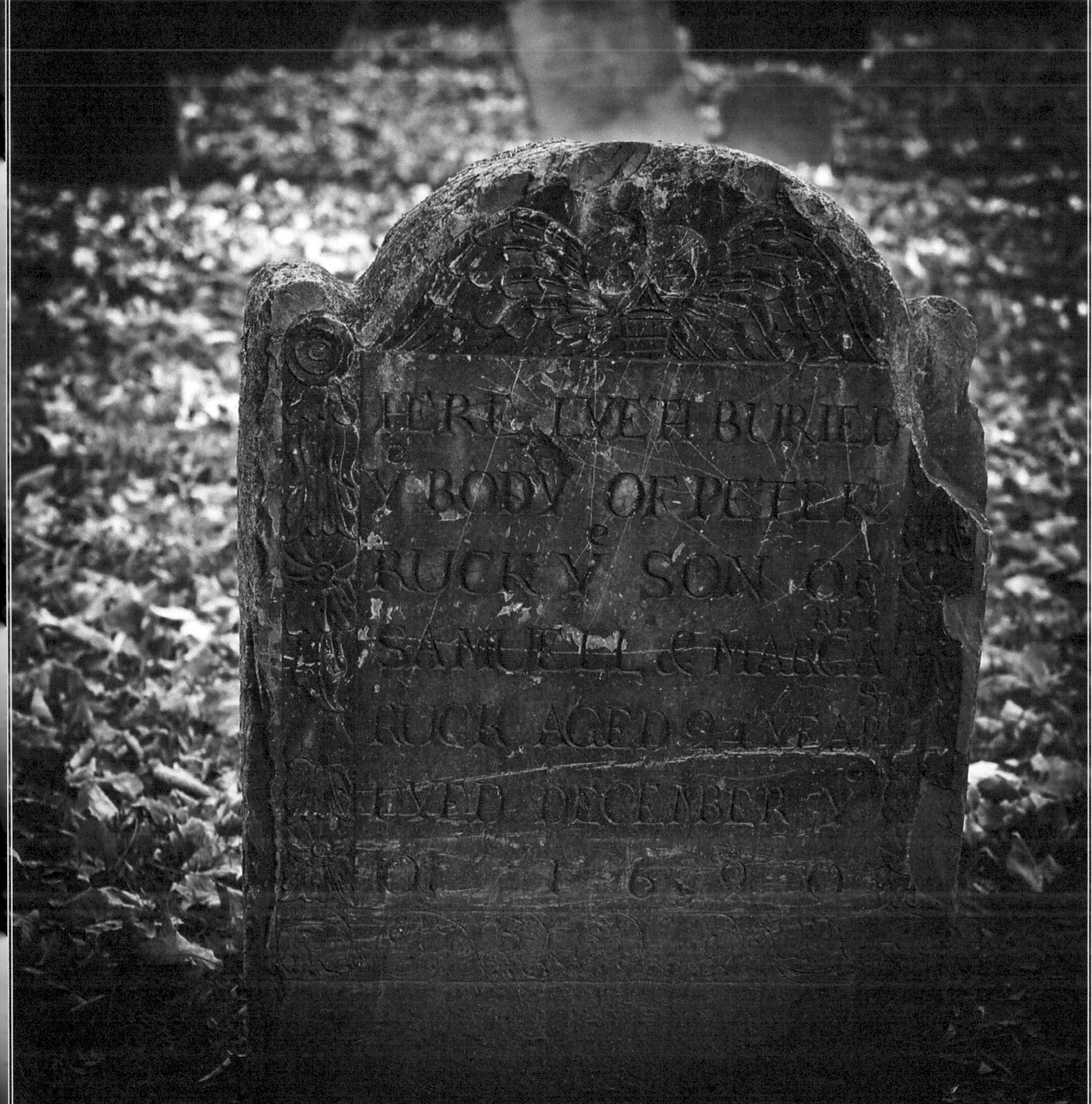

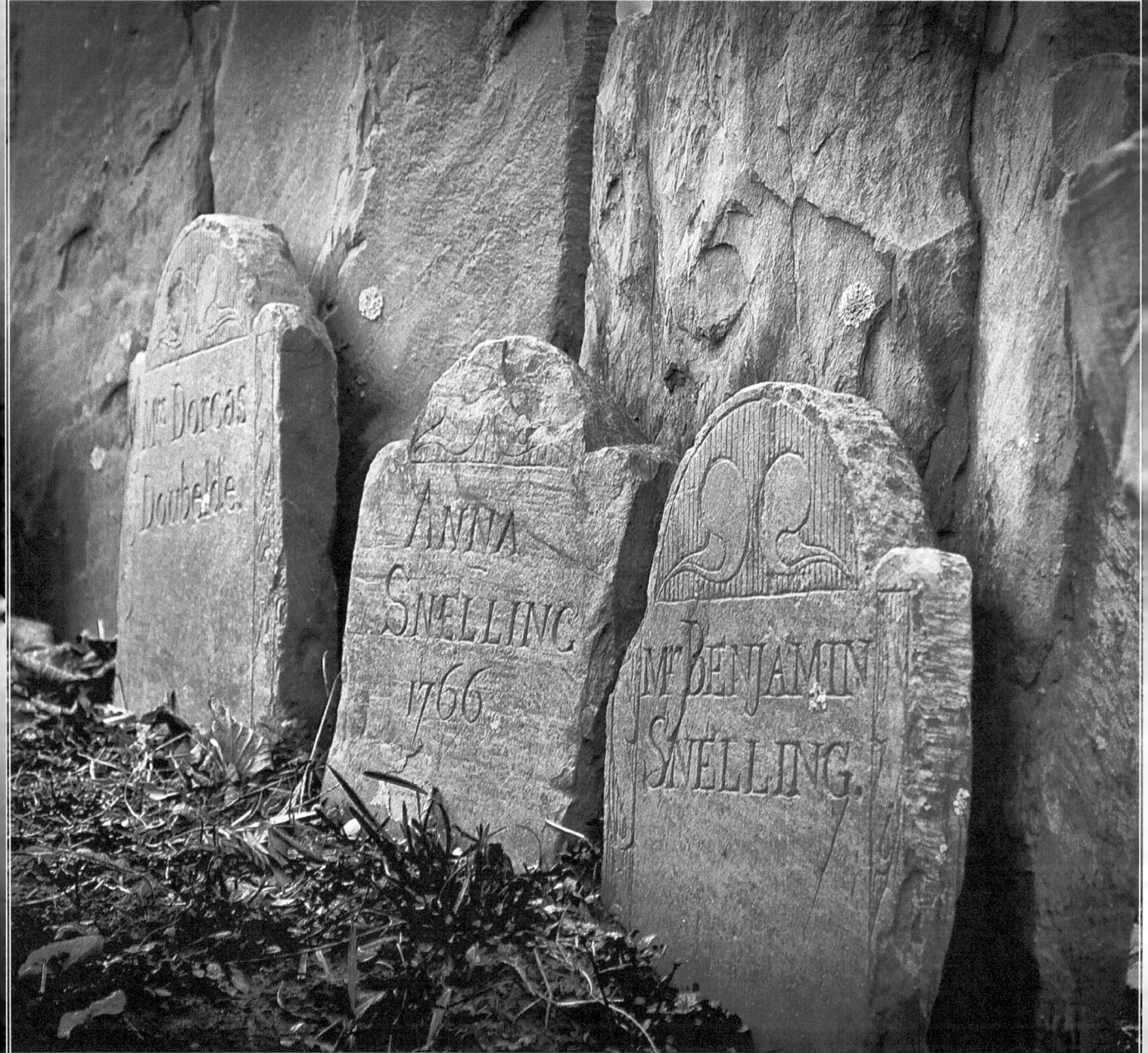

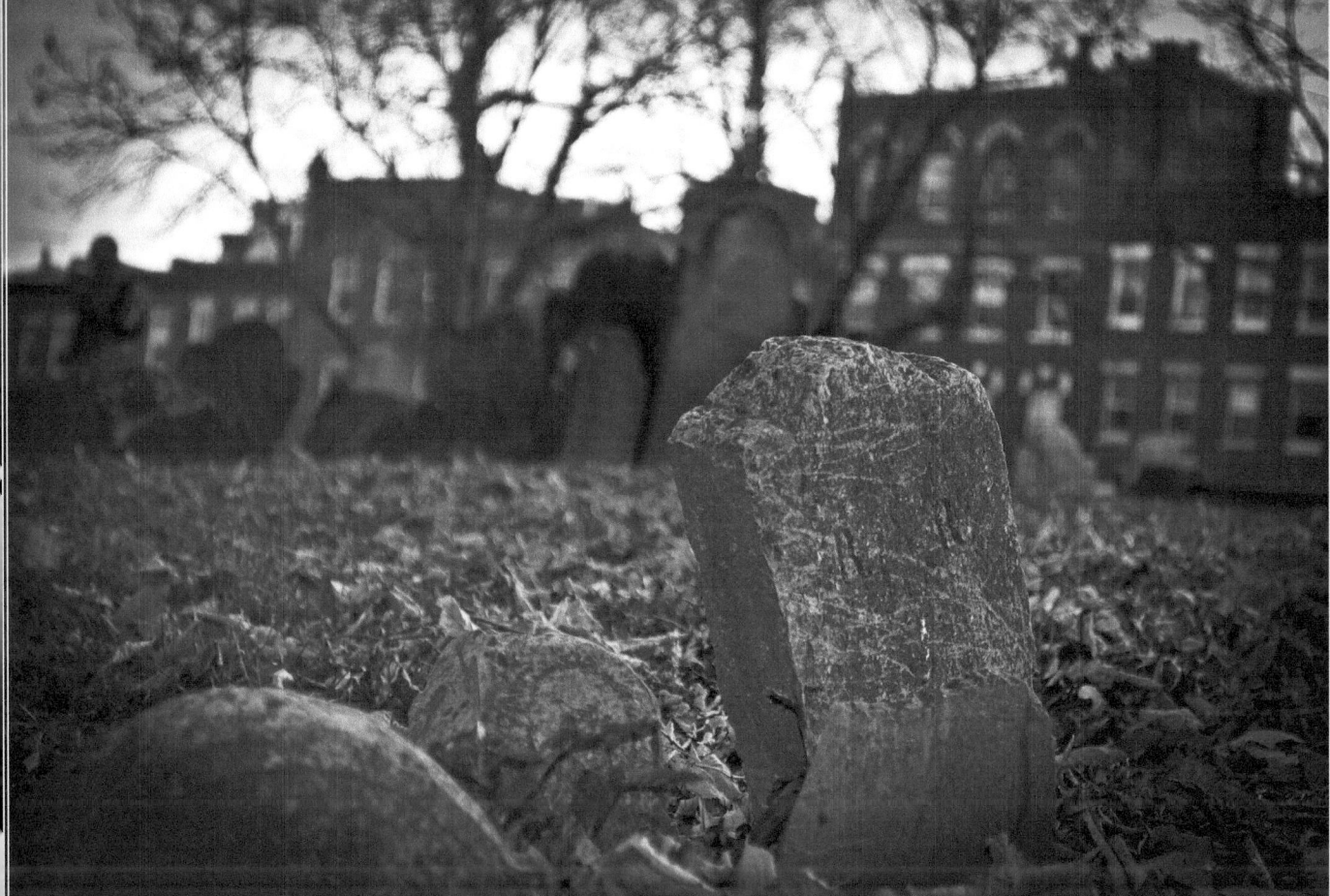

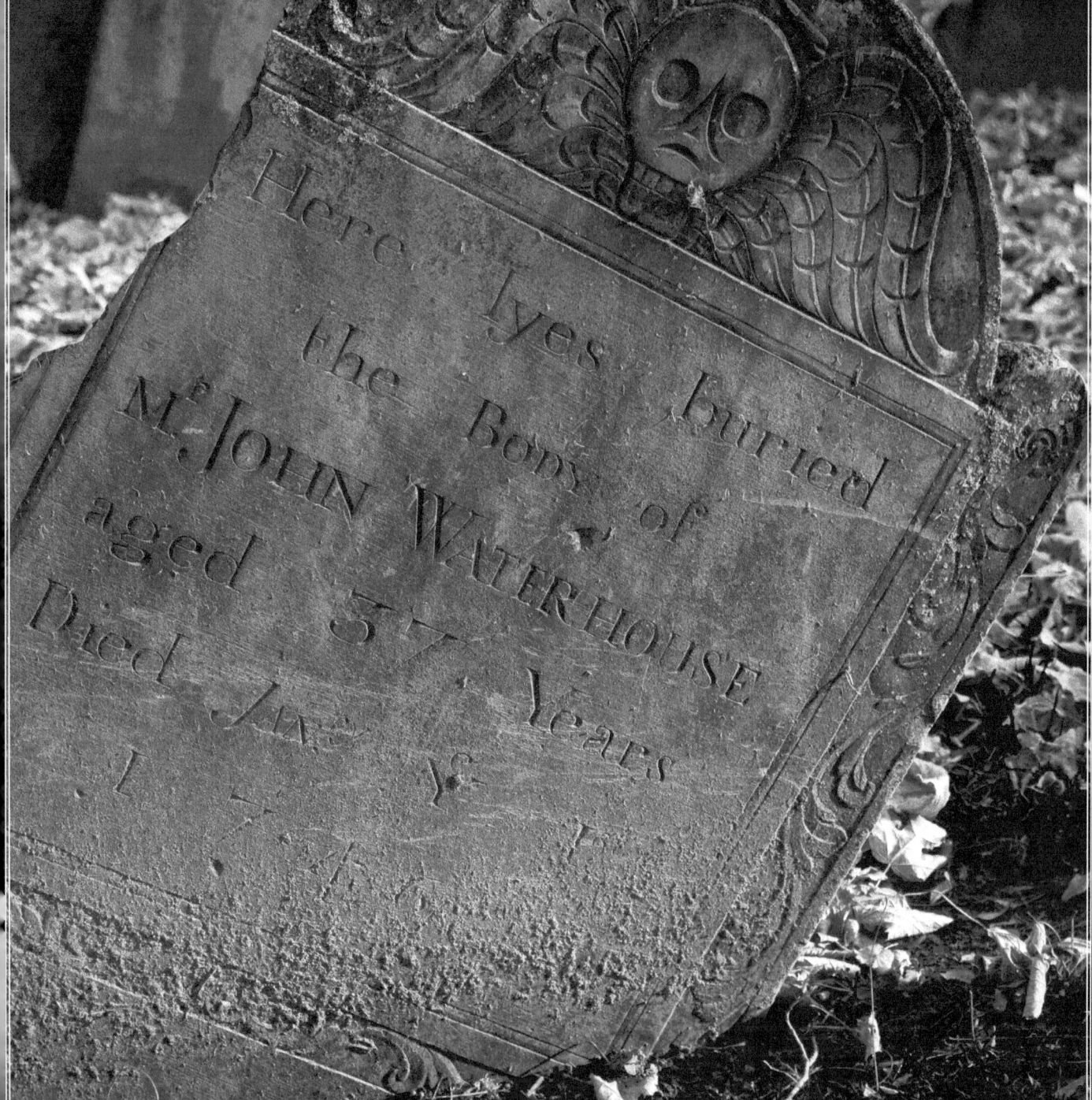

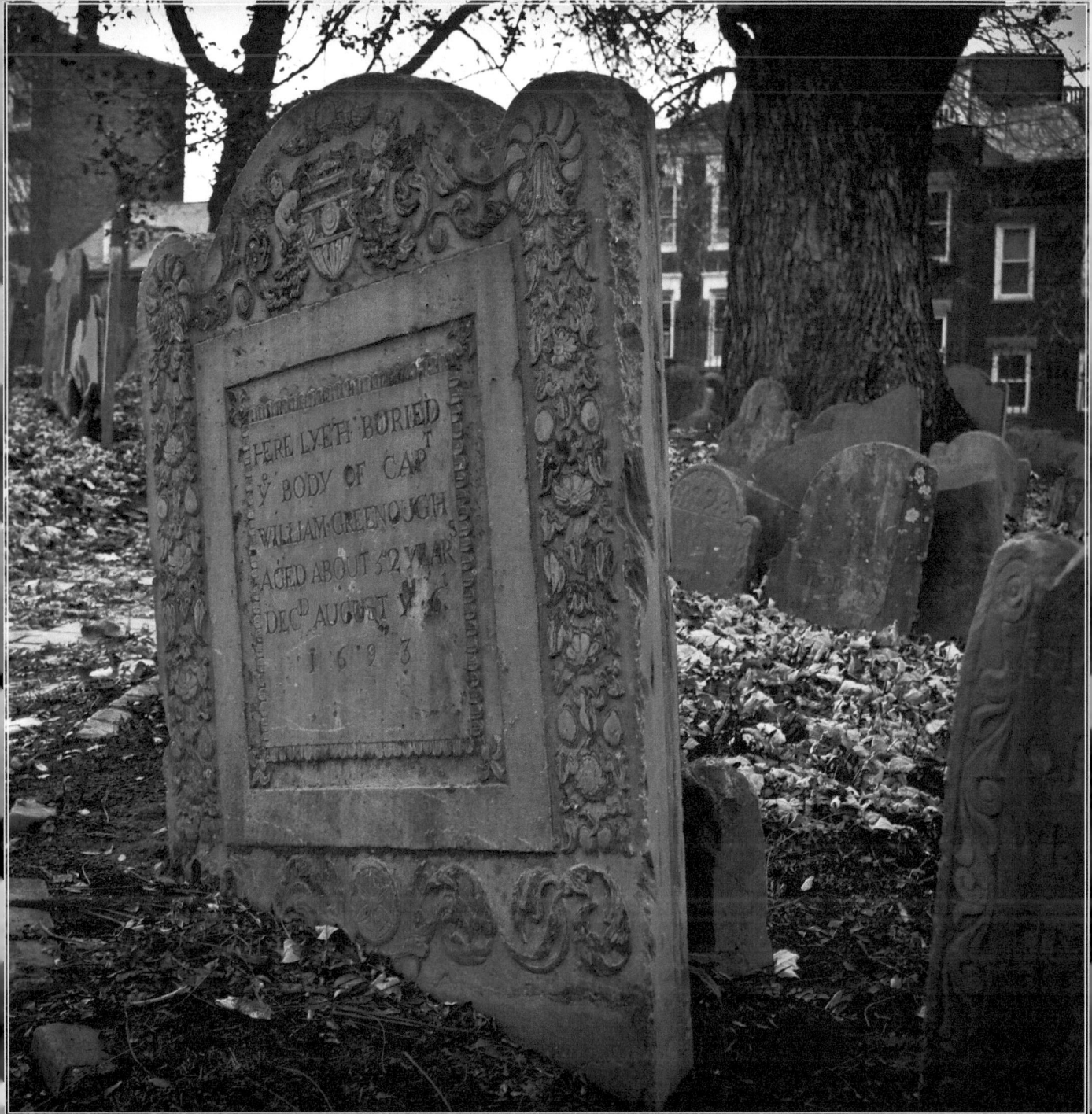

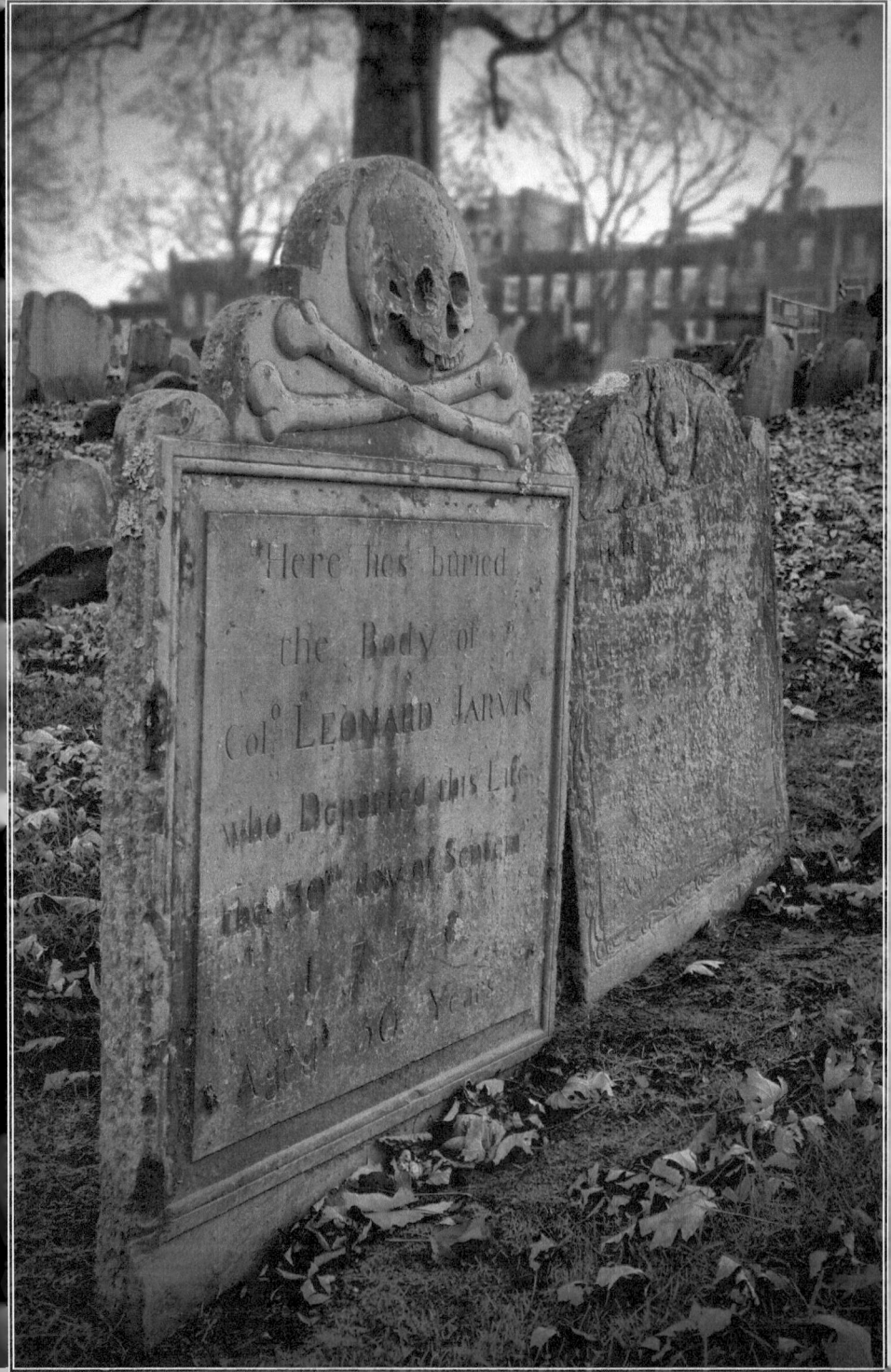

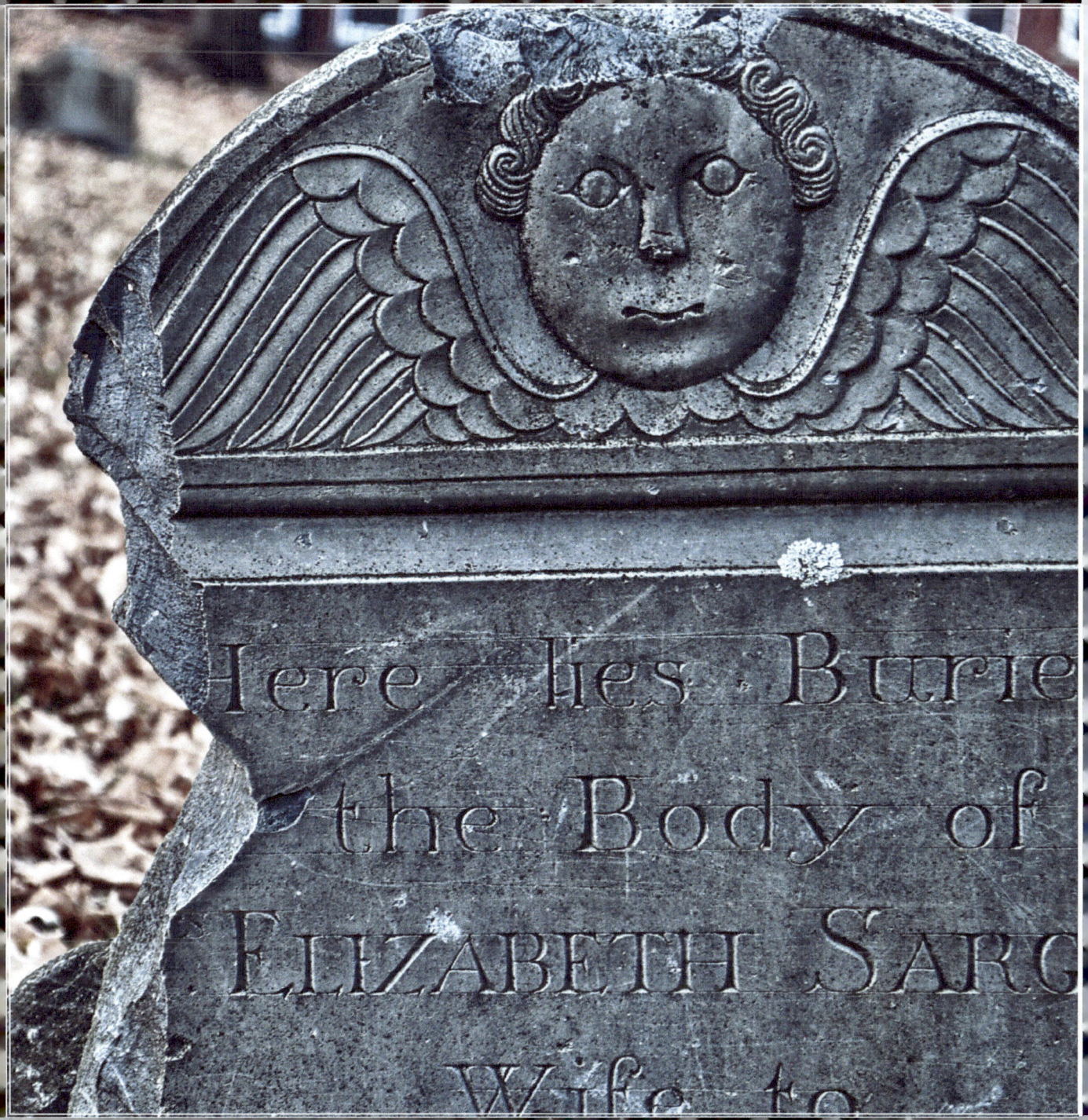

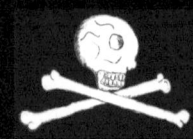

Sacred to the Memory of MR THOMAS GILMAN
who departed this life April 12th 1807 Aged 42 years.

"Stop my friends, and in a mirror see
What you, though e'er so healthy, soon must be.
Beauty, with all her rosebuds, paints each face;
Approaching death will strip you of each grace."

In Memory of MISS REBECCA PERKINS, dau'r of
Mr. James & Mrs. Sally Perkins who died March 16,
1802, aged 19 years, 7 months & 13 days.

"My friends and parents, do not mourn,
Nor drop one tear now I am gone;
Where I am gone I am at rest,
Pray think me numbered with the blest."

Sacred to the Memory of MR RICHARD ROBERTS son to Mr. Richard &
Mrs. Mercy Roberts who departed this life June 16, 1812, 26.

"My glass is run, my life is spent, My earthly temple was but lent;
Why should I wish a length of years, In such a vale of tears?"

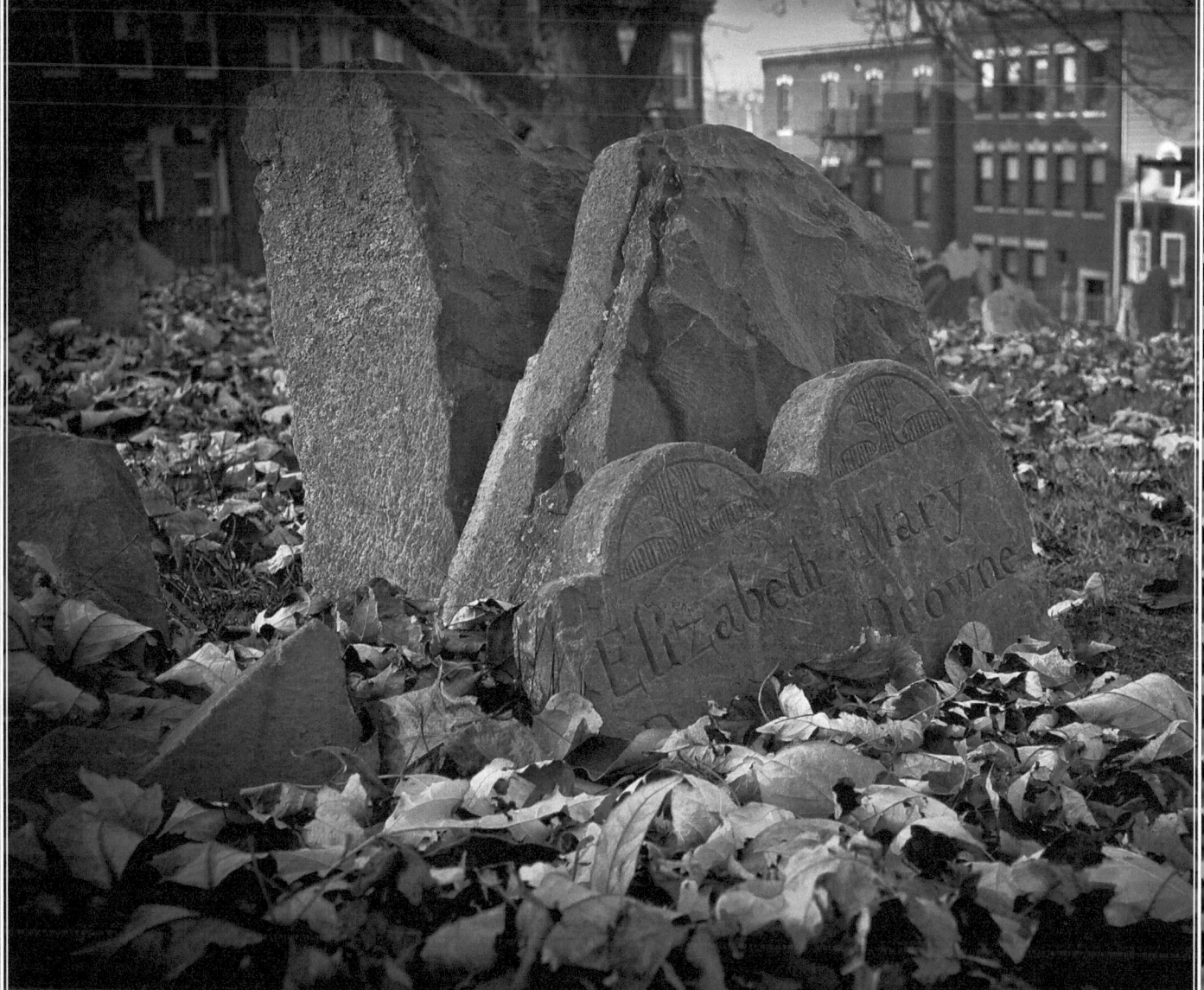

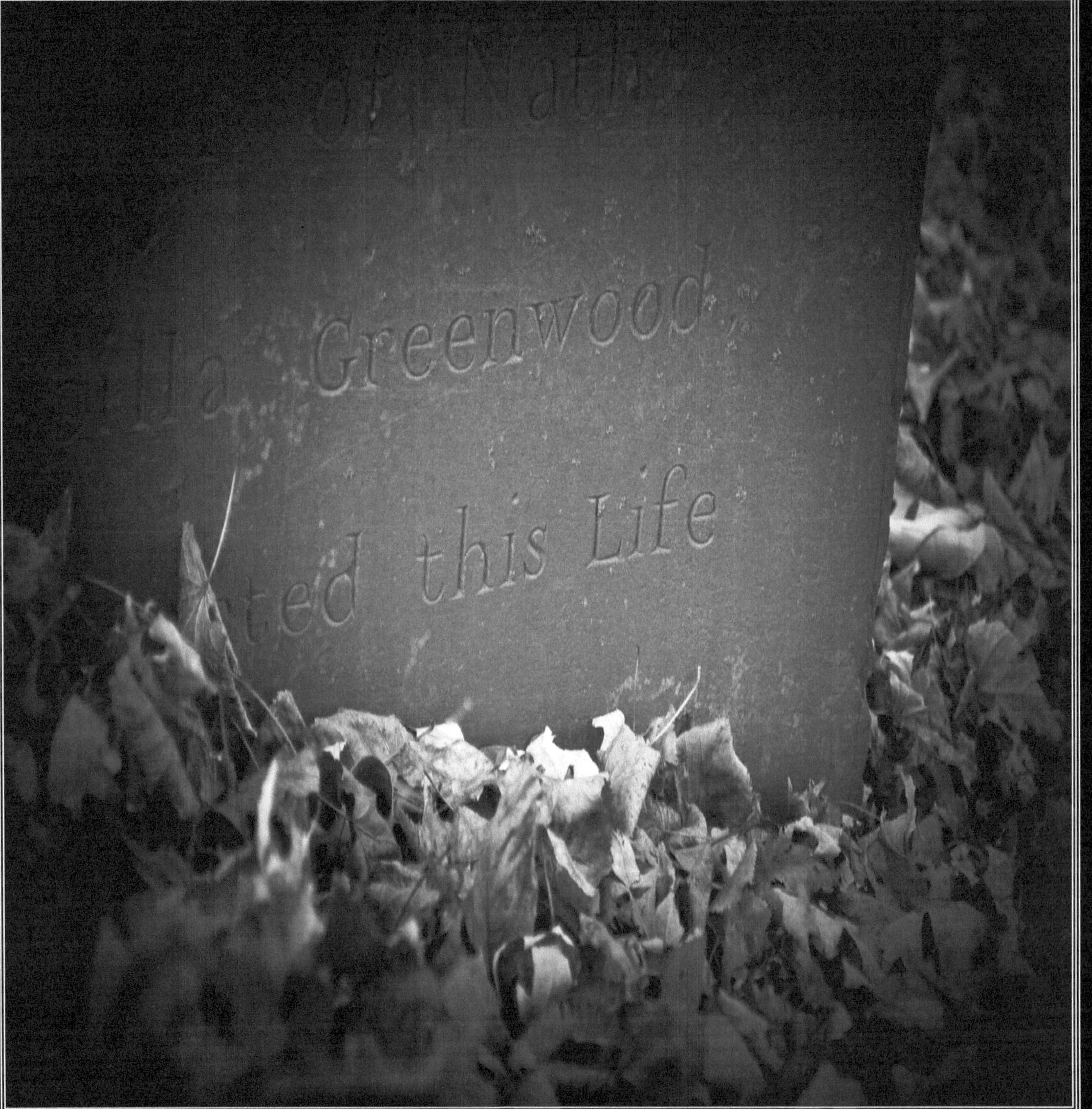

of Nath

Greenwood,

ted this Life

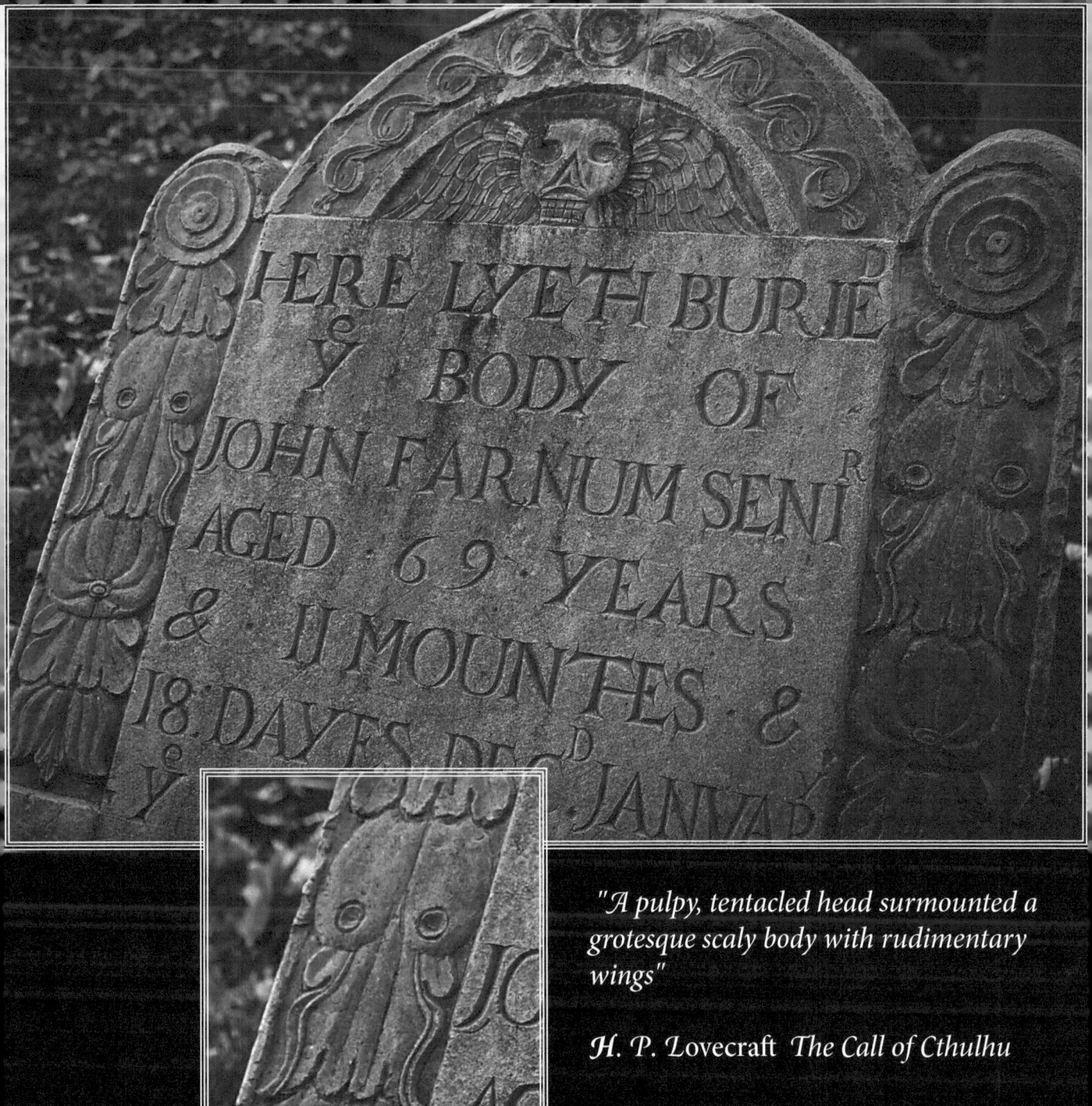

HERE LYETH BURIE
Yᵉ BODY OF
JOHN FARNUM SENIᴿ
AGED · 69 · YEARS
& II MOUNTES &
18 DAYES DECᴰ
Yᵉ JANVAᴿᵞ

"A pulpy, tentacled head surmounted a grotesque scaly body with rudimentary wings"

H. P. Lovecraft *The Call of Cthulhu*

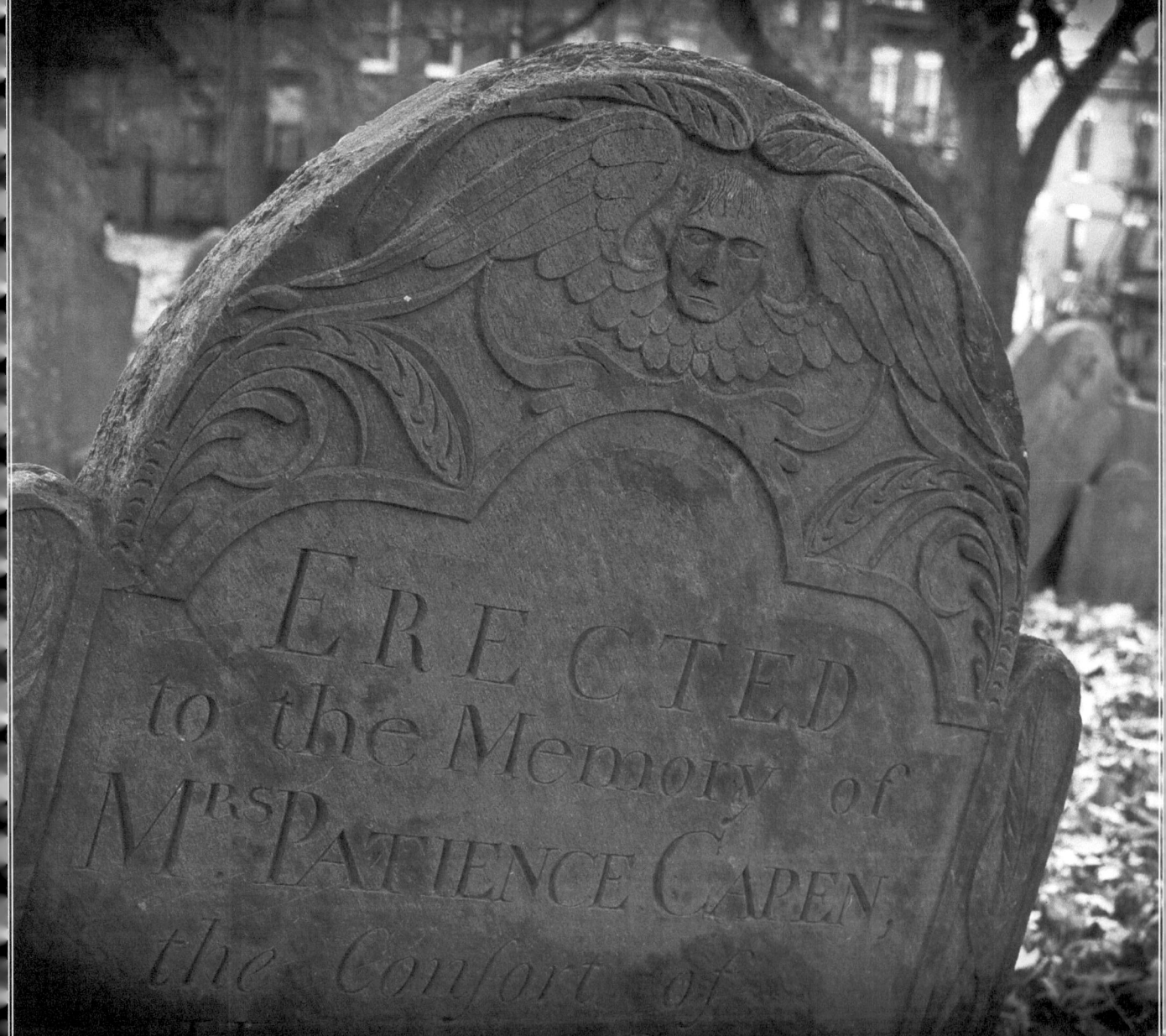

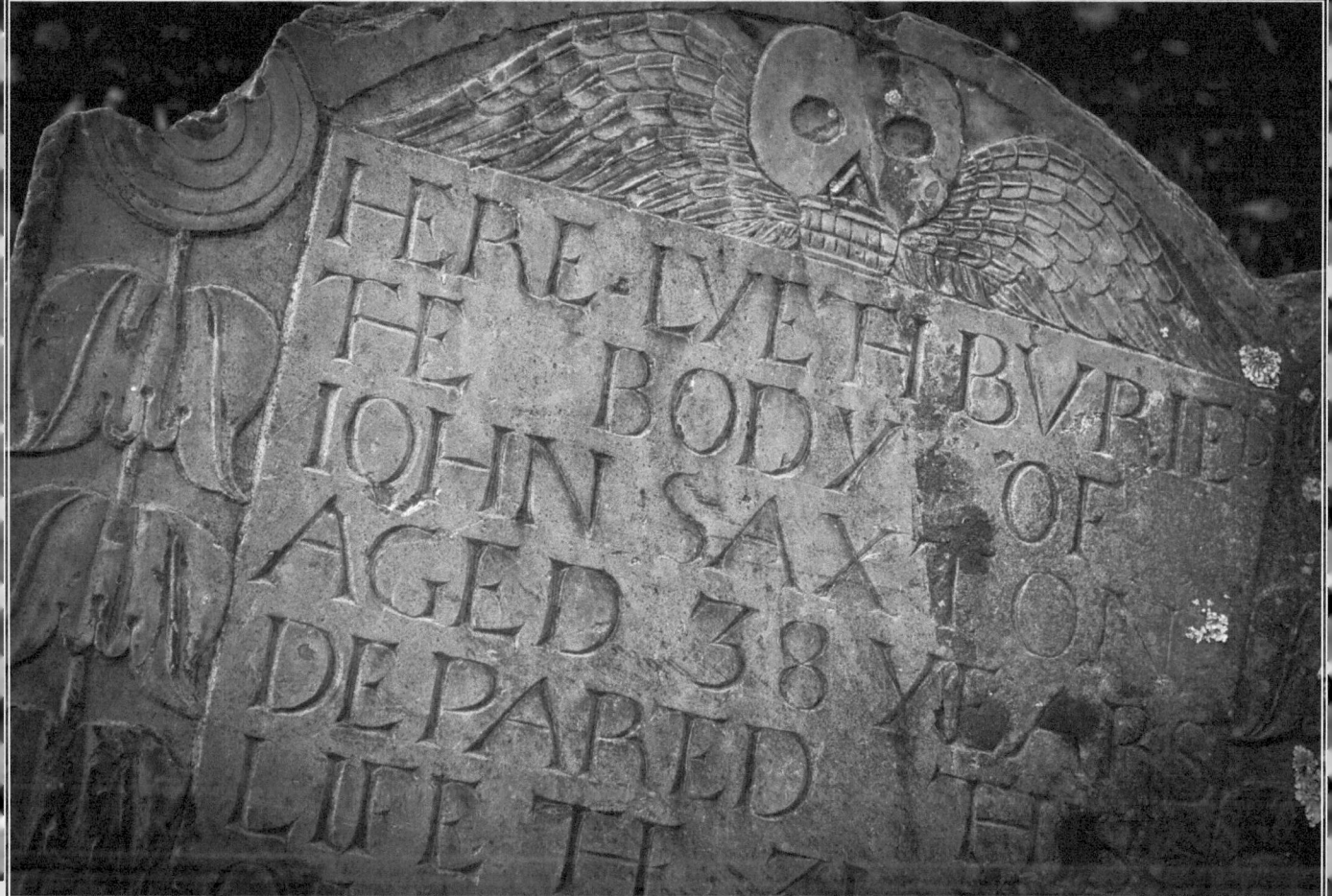

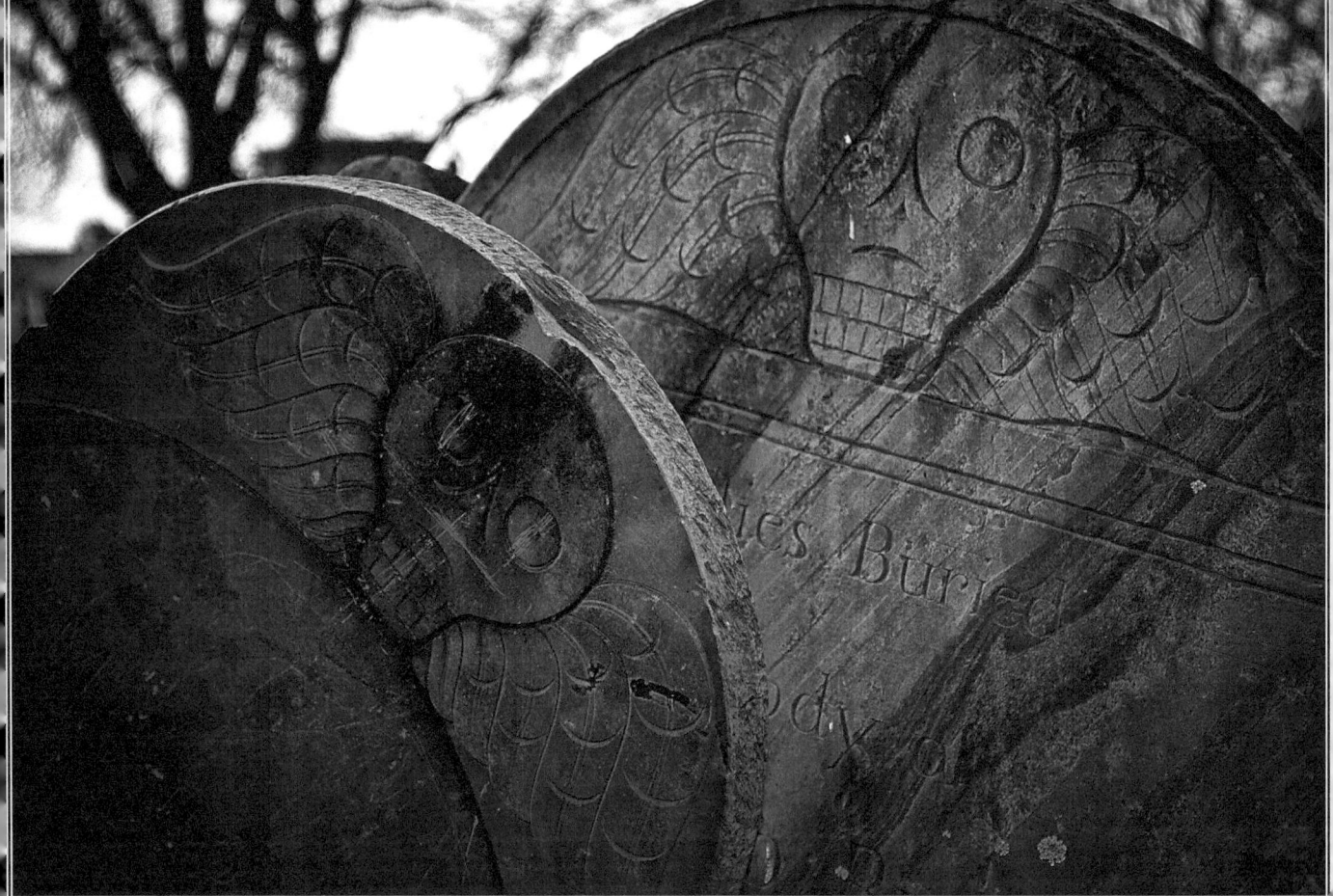

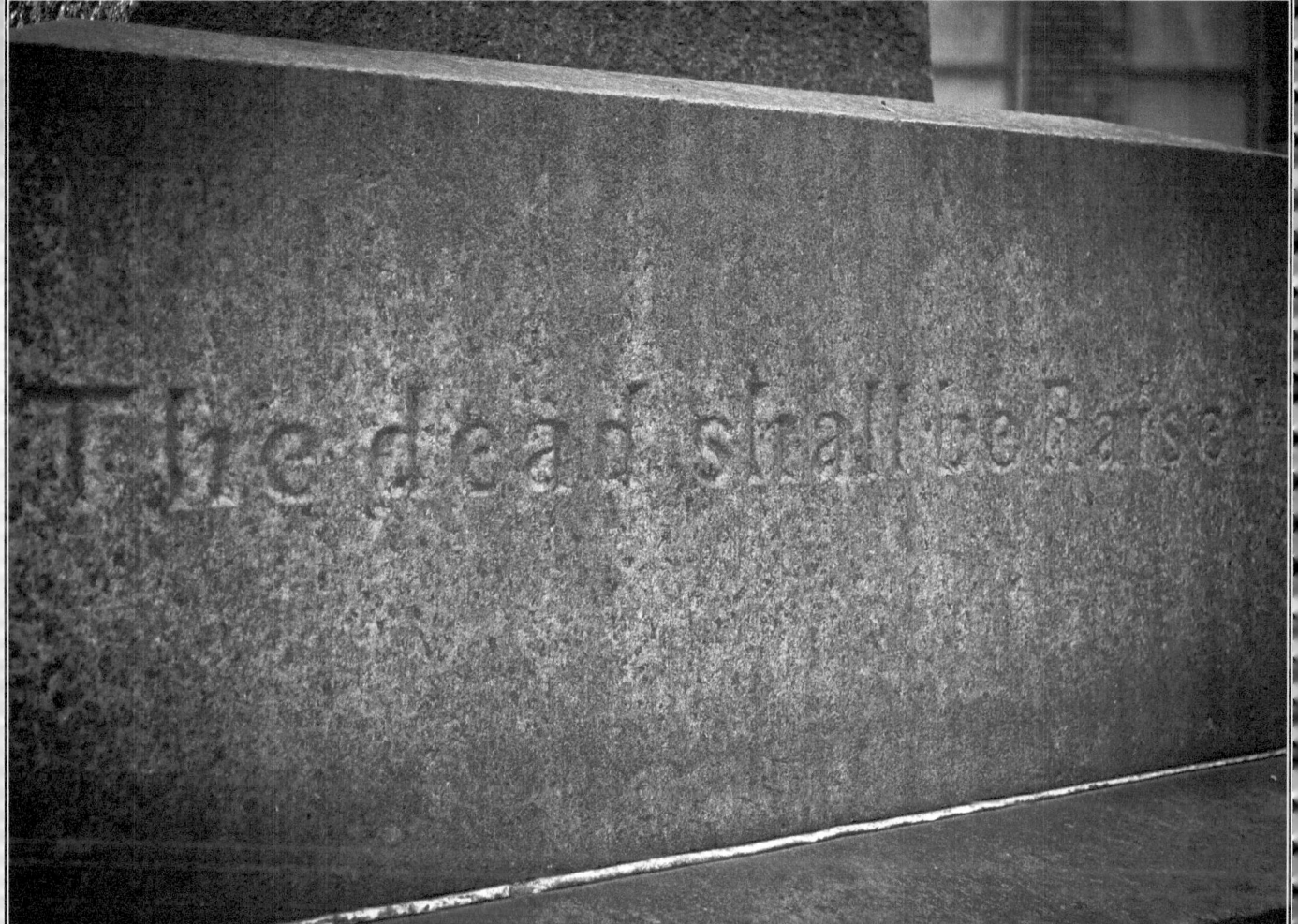

...th near
...Old England Nor
...) who departed his Life
the 23d Day of August 1798
...in the 23d Year of his Age.

In Peace here rests a Traveler's Dust,
His Journey's at an End,
He priz'd Esteem ... the Just,
A Censure from ... Friend

Broke loose from Time's ... Chains
And Earth's ... claims ... on
To range at ... in ... the ...
Of radiant Worlds to ...

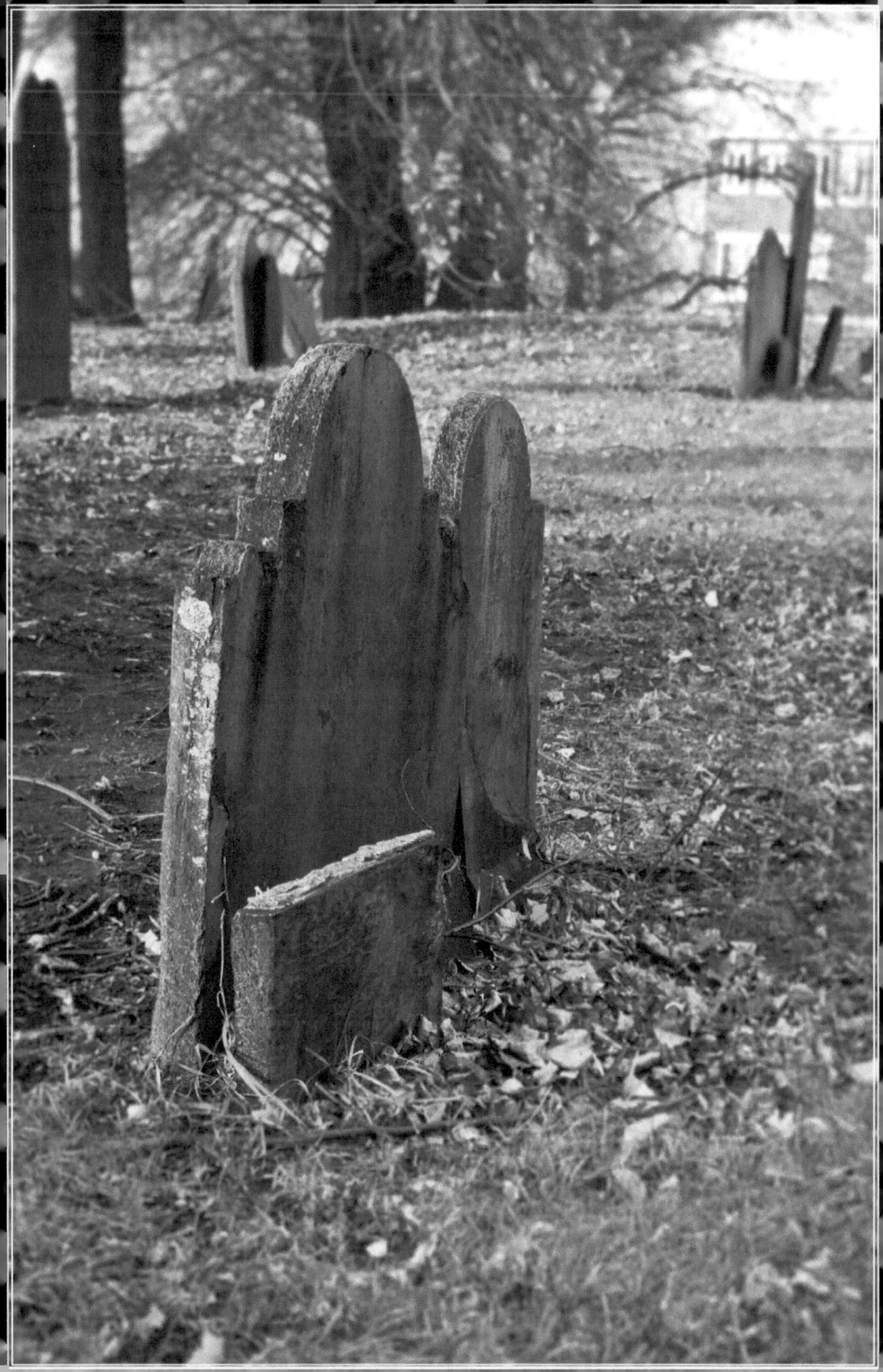

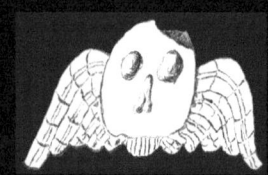

In Memory of MRS ANN CLOUGH Wife of Mr. Samuel
Clough Died April ye 2nd 1772 - aged 52 years.

"My parents gone. Greate Heaven
O tell me where -
Where may I drop my unaffected tear
In fillial gratitude - Where may I weep
In gratefull silence - Lull my soul to sleep.
May I awake in heaven & find her there
Where endless raptures qwell each rising care."

Sacred to the Memory of MR ELIJAH CORLEW
who departed this life May 25th, 1804, aged 31 years also, his infant child.

"Lo! Soft remembrance drops the piteous tear
And dearest friendship stands a mourner here."

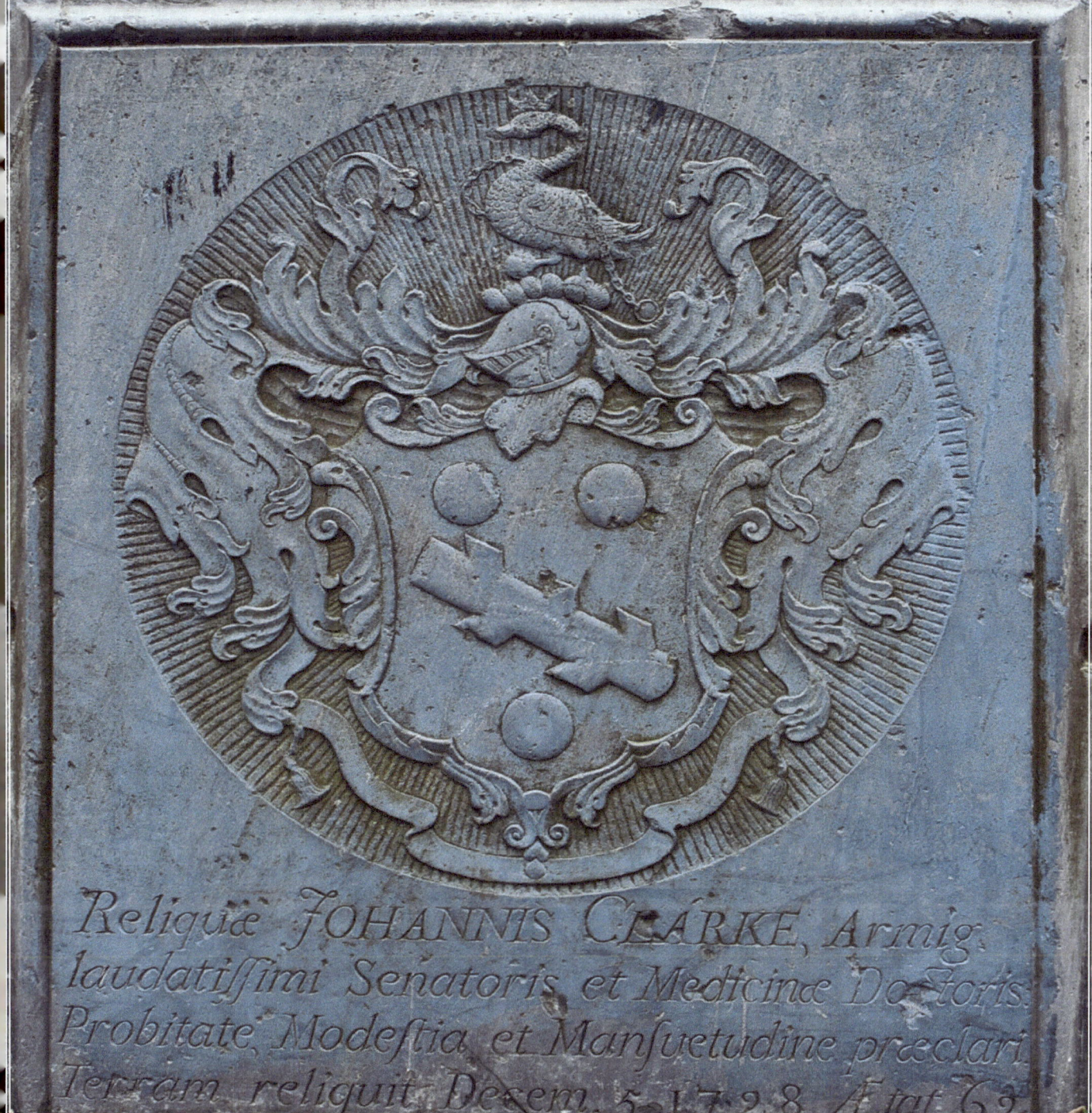

Reliquæ JOHANNIS CLARKE, Armig.
laudatiſſimi Senatoris et Medicinæ Doſtoris.
Probitate, Modeſtia et Manſuetudine præclari.
Terram reliquit Decem. 5. 1728. Ætat 69.

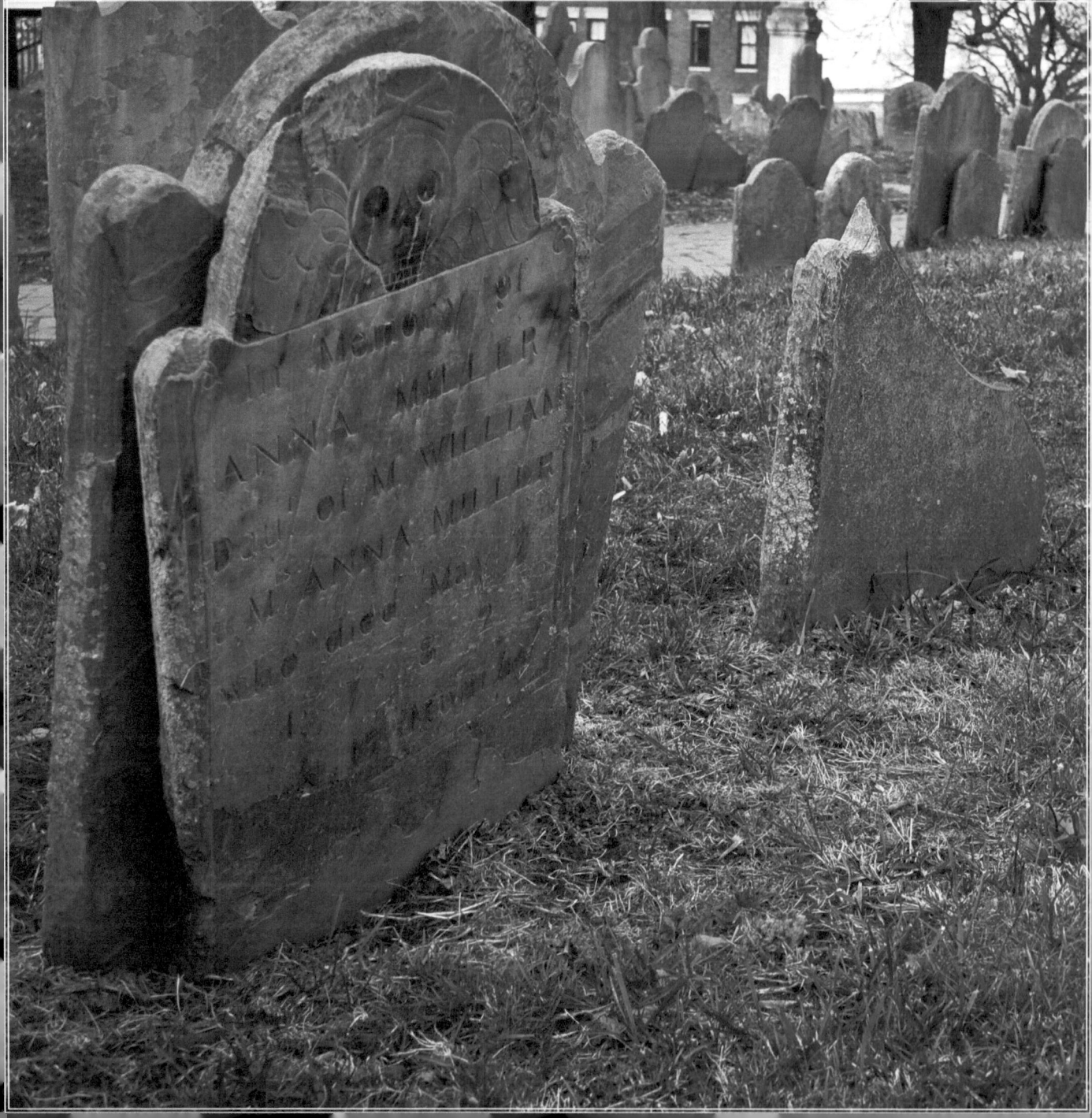

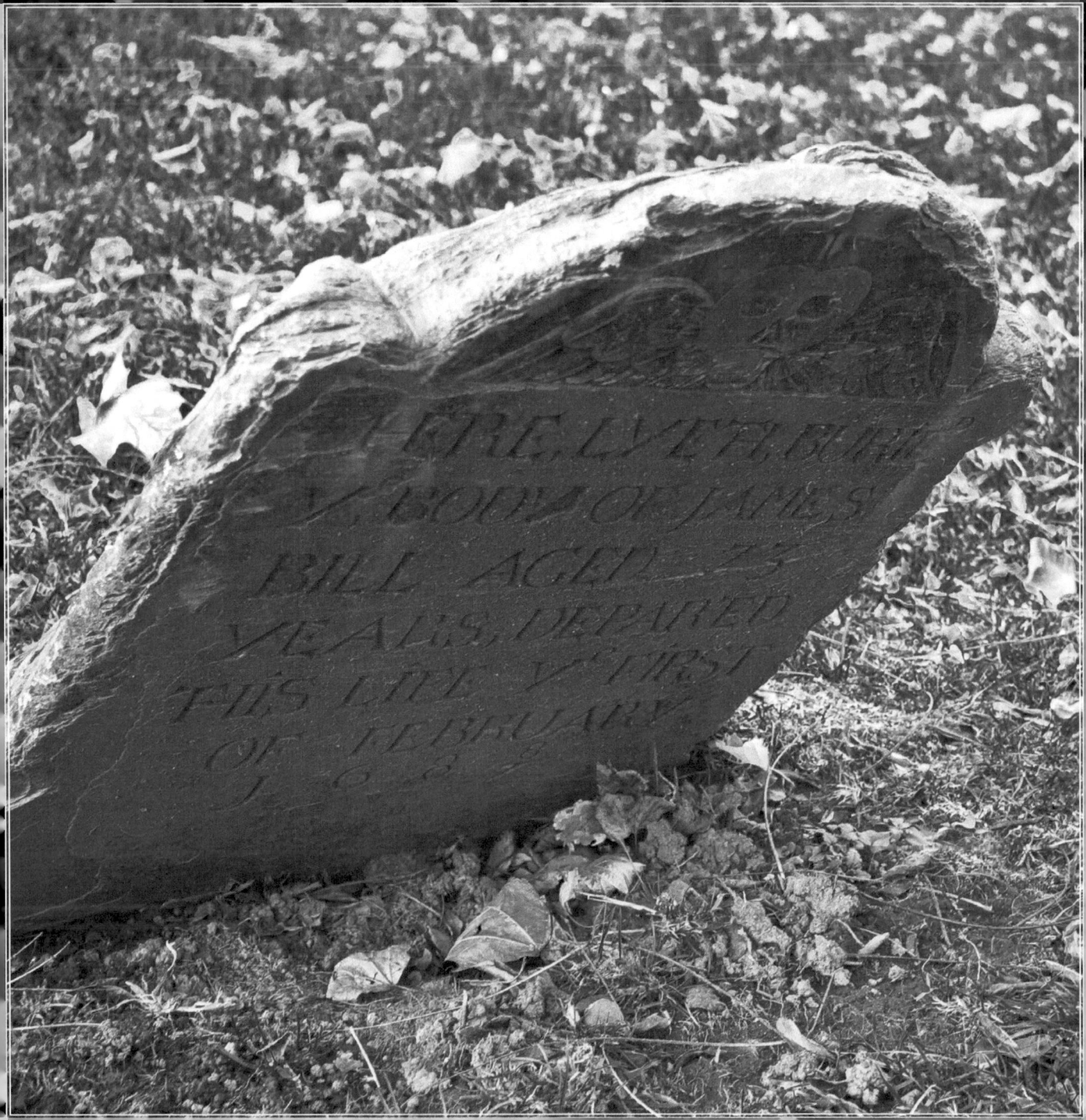

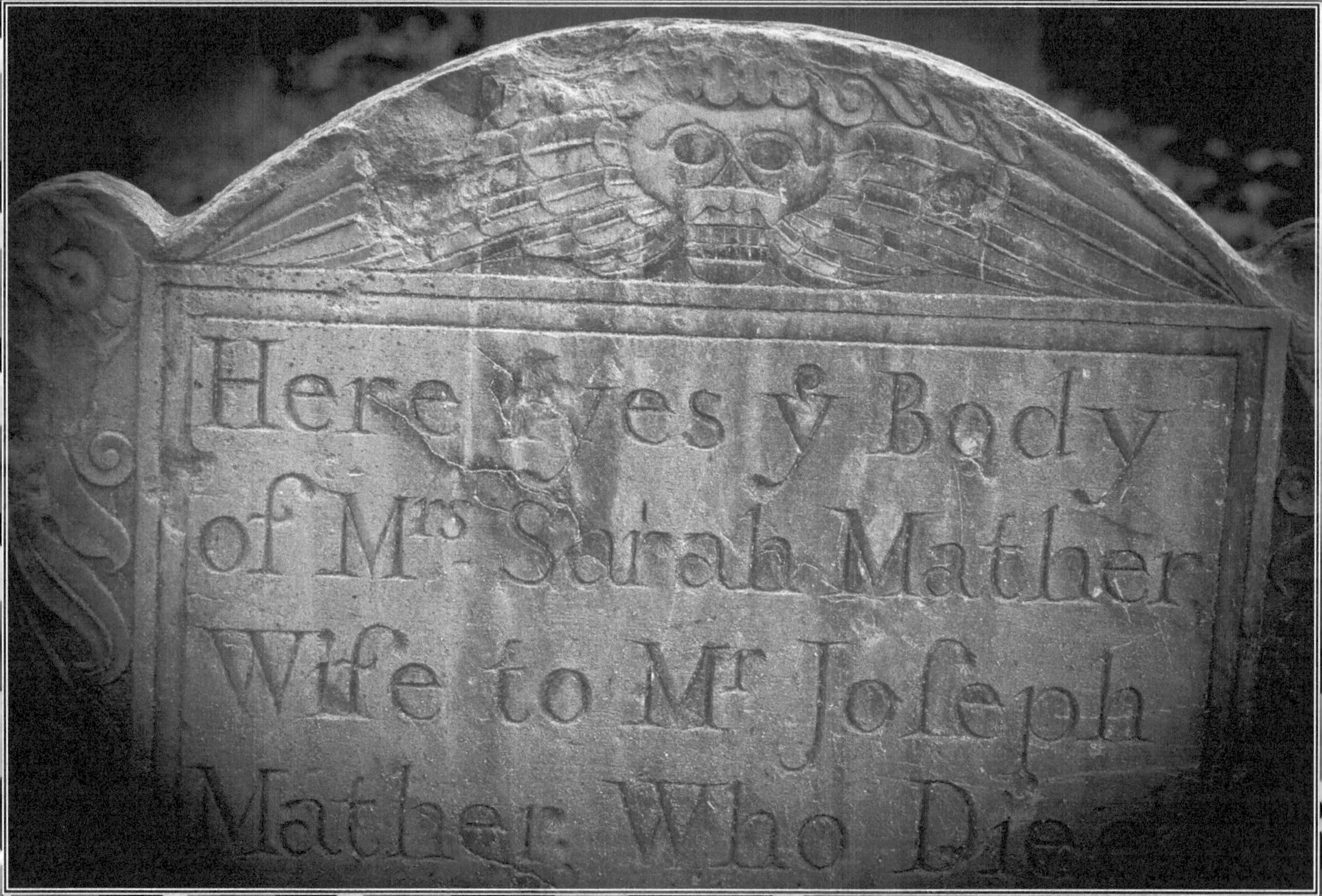

Here lyes y Body
of Mrs Sarah Mather
Wife to Mr Joseph
Mather Who Die

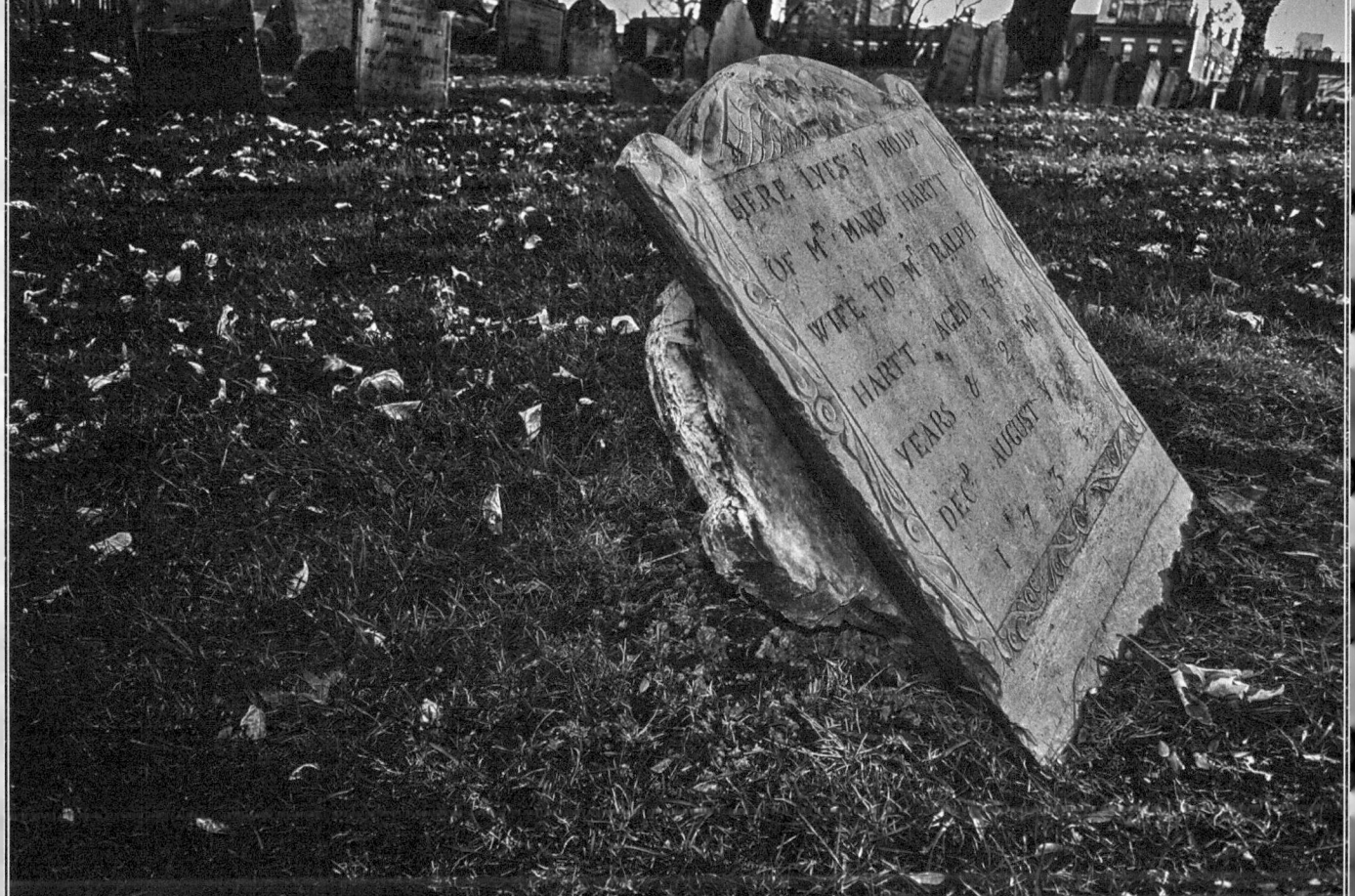

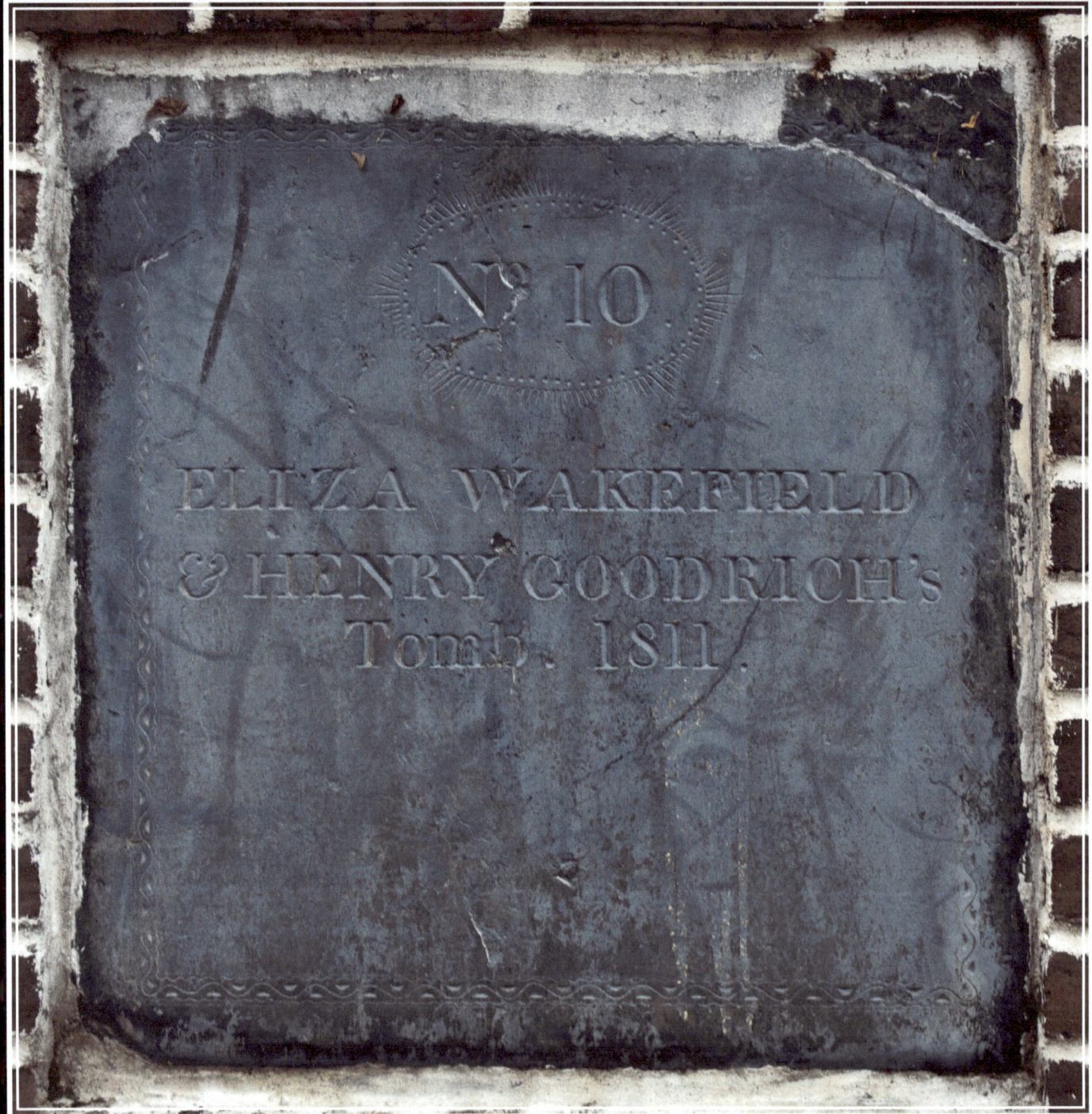

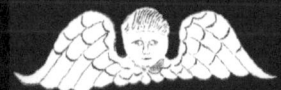

About the Author

Vincent-louis Apruzzese is a multi-media professional working in graphic design, video post production and internet design. He lives in Montréal, Québec.

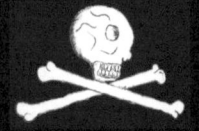

The information in this book was taken from personal experiences, cityofbosoton.gov, Wikipedia, freedomtrail.org, genealogytrails.com, *Memorials of the Dead* by Thomas Bridgman (1852), as well as some H.P. Lovecraft for good measure.

Personal Remarks

Growing up in historic Boston, Massachusetts in the 1960s, I had the good fortune to have access to some of the oldest and most renowned graveyards in the United States. I took full advantage of them. For me, they are restful places filled with history, untold stories and wonderful works of art. It is easy to forget how special they are.

I was always in awe of Copp's Hill Burying Ground, having first visited there at as young boy with an unmarried aunt. One of my favorite authors, H.P. Lovecraft, mentioned the cemetery in one of his best known short stories, *Pickman's Model*. One of the stones even has what looks like the inspiration for Lovecraft's ghastly creation, the Cthulhu. Of all the old burial places in the city, this is the one that most strikes a chord with me.

Even though I might prefer a more out of the way and hidden boneyard for my remains, I can't say the idea of digging a hole and hiding myself under Copp's Hill for eternity doesn't hold a certain appeal.

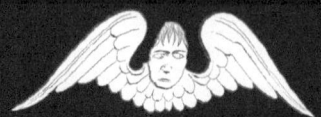

About the Photos

*A*ll the photos in this book were taken with the aid of Boston artist and my longtime friend, Ralph Hodgdon. Oddly, this was his first visit to the burial ground, even though he lives within walking distance. Some of the photos are retouched to remove graffiti from the artistry of the engravings. I don't wish to give more attention to those who think they have the right to scratch their names on historic stones.

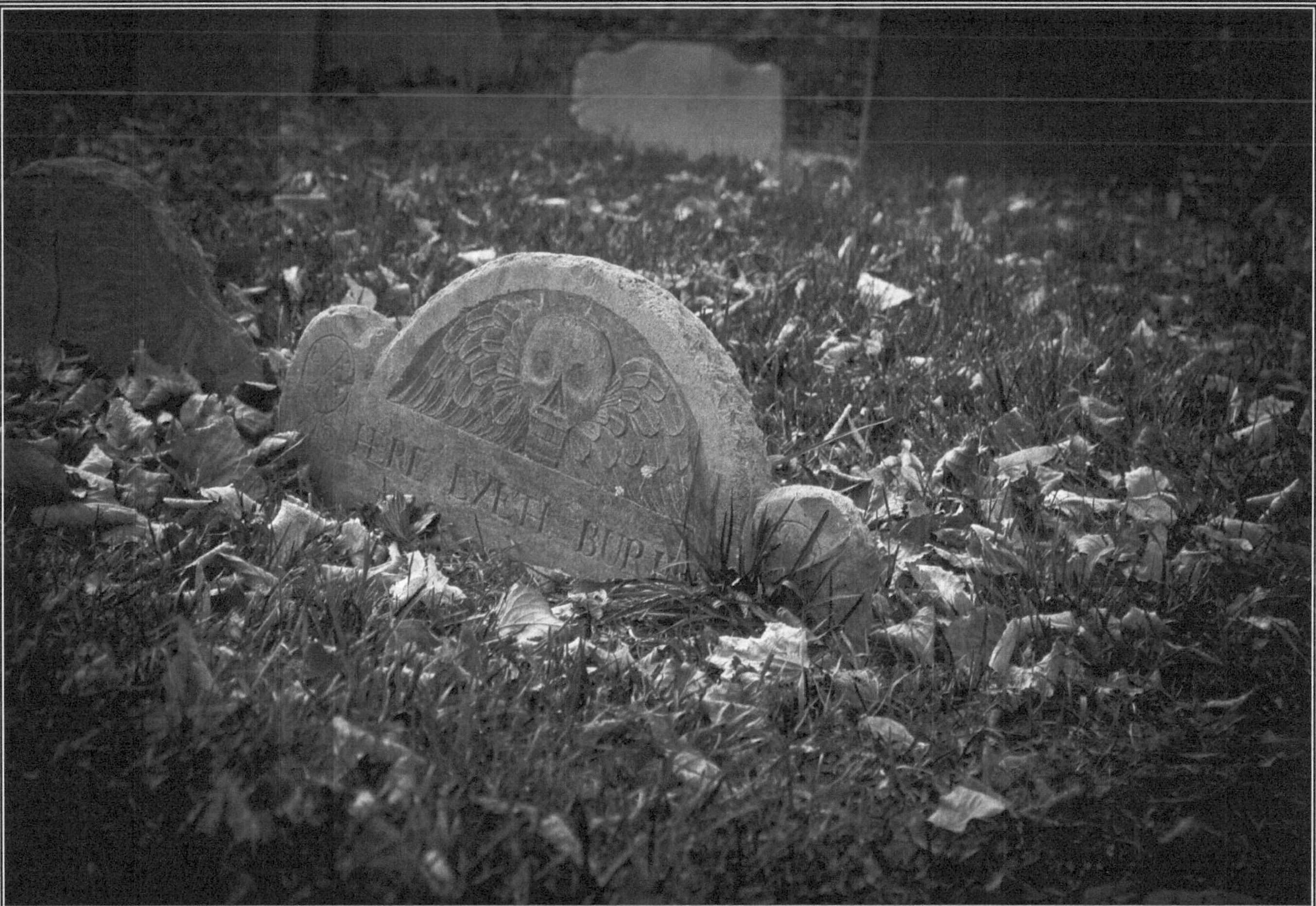

Dedicated to J.E. Reeves
with whom I have spent many an hour in such places.

Photography, design, illustrations & text by Vincent-louis Apruzzese.
Edited by Arthur Dion & Denis Leclerc
© 2012 Vincent-louis Apruzzese

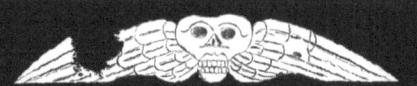

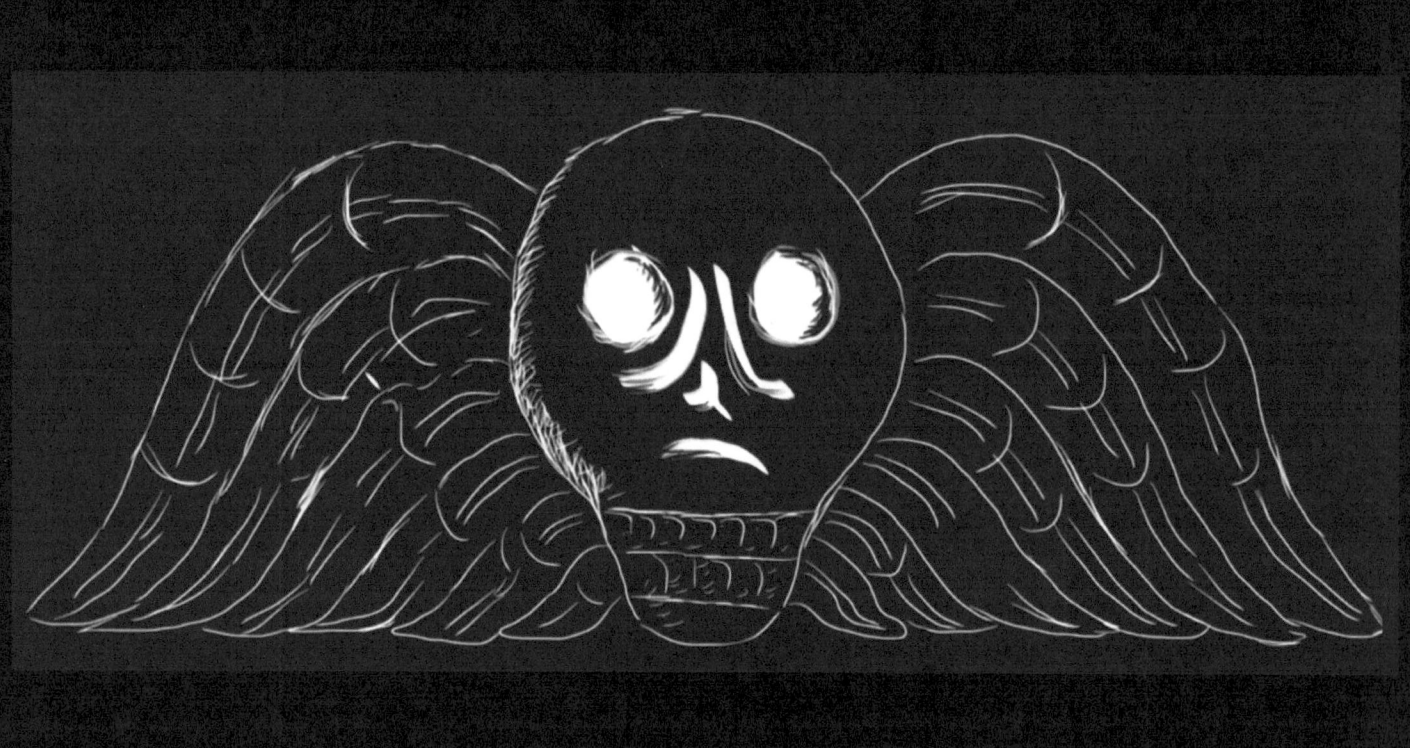